CW00943792

MEET ME IN THE KITCHEN

Bedsit, Farm or Stately Home

MEET ME IN THE KITCHEN

Bedsit, Farm or Stately Home

Betty Thornton

ATHENA PRESS
LONDON

MEET ME IN THE KITCHEN
Bedsit, Farm or Stately Home
Copyright © Betty Thornton 2009

All Rights Reserved

ISBN 978 1 84748 617 2

First published 2009 by
ATHENA PRESS
Queen's House, 2 Holly Road
Twickenham TW1 4EG
United Kingdom

Printed for Athena Press

To my dear parents, GEF and DLF.
If only you could have known all the story.

Preface

It is 5.45 p.m. on 29 July 1981 and some 900 million people worldwide have been sitting in front of their television sets for the entire day watching the wedding of HRH the Prince of Wales and Lady Diana Spencer take place. It has been a day filled with pageant, spectacle, tradition and emotion. But now people are leaving their sets, making meals and having a drink or a cup of tea.

But I am standing in the basement kitchen of Broadlands, Romsey, trying to create a moment of total isolation despite the house almost crackling with tension, as it has been since 7 a.m. this morning. The security has been checked and rechecked by detectives, there are experts on hidden cameras, infrared cameras, night-time binoculars and also dog handlers. Men are scouring the grounds; radio telephones are in use everywhere. The latest scare is just over – five local boys climbed the estate wall and dropped into the grounds but were seized immediately. Last night two French reporters were overheard in the Tudor Rose pub, plotting to swim the river in snorkel outfits from the town bridge. They planned to emerge from the River Test opposite the Portico where the lawn comes down to the river, hoping to photograph the newly-weds looking out of the Portico bedroom tonight. That plan has been well and truly scotched!

But I am not affected by any of this at the moment. I am standing at the long wooden table in the kitchen (scrubbed down every night) and thinking my own thoughts. I have checked all my preparations for the light and delicate meal that is planned for tonight and I'm saying to myself, 'Betty, however did it come about that aged fifty-five you are standing here in Broadlands kitchen, waiting to cook the wedding-night meal of the Prince and Princess of Wales? You were an art student in wartime, became a textile designer and married a fellow student, a sculptor. And all of this would have come as such a tremendous shock if it could have been foretold.'

But at this quiet moment I am not nervous, because there have been many weekends over the past nine months when I have cooked for Prince Charles and Lady Diana and I have got to know their favourite foods. In fact, the week-end before the wedding we had a jolly conference around this table and decided to have the greatest possible flexibility in the timing of the meals; we decided on the menus themselves and on the need for informality.

Lord and Lady Romsey are in London for the wedding and have left the house for three days to the newly-weds. There are just four of the Broadlands house staff present: myself; Vic, the butler, and his wife Rose, the housekeeper; and Bryan, the footman. At the present moment, the royal detectives, the valet, the dresser and security men are in the staff dining room, finishing a hurried meal. But at the very heart of the house – the entrance hall, salon and the bedrooms – all is peaceful and no one would guess that there is so much tension and activity here in the basement. There have been moments of humour peeping through in this tense atmosphere. We had all been asked not to use the phones if possible, but Jane, the head groom, had rushed into the kitchen saying, 'I shall have to use the phone to contact the vet. Panda must have some udder cream for his sunburn!' Panda was one of the piebald drum horses of the Household Cavalry who spend a summer's break at Broadlands and this cream was perfect for his fair skin.

We have all been up and about since 7 a.m. making preparations and taking messages, but also dashing up to the nursery sitting room on the top floor to watch TV, accompanied by the '*pish pish*' of the steam iron as Rose attends to last-minute ironing. The day goes by quickly and the Prince and Princess have boarded the train for their journey to Romsey. The royal car, which has been parked at the North Door all day, has left for the station. The townsfolk of Romsey and many others – an estimated 100,000 – are lining the streets and the world's press is clamouring at the gates. As 6 p.m. approaches, messages start coming through to the house on the police radio telephones.

I glance round the kitchen once more, then hurry up the stairs to the butler's pantry in time to see on the small TV, balanced on the draining board, that the heavy wrought-iron gates are opening. The crowd is ecstatic – waving, cheering; the police hold them back and the car glides through. The gates close and, for the world, it is the very last glimpse of the couple. But the four of us look at each other and say, 'This is it!' There are three nights and two days of great excitement ahead – a moment in history – so we hurry to the Marble Entrance Hall. It is to be my privilege to open the front door and make the first greeting, as Vic and Bryan will be outside to deal with the gates and the luggage. There is just time to hold up a hand in greeting to all the estate employees invited to stand at the inner gates – then, suddenly, they are here! I open the door, curtsey and say, 'Welcome, your Royal Highnesses.' We are quite tearful.

Prince Charles says, 'Isn't she beautiful? And I am a lucky man.' They ask, 'How did it all look? Has Vic got it on video for us?' They hurry off, arms around each other, to walk down the steep stretch of lawn to the peace of the River Test flowing by.

I return to the kitchen, treading on air, and wait to be given the time of the meal. It is a perfect evening – dusky blue sky, stars – and the view from the Portico steps is idyllic.

Vic hurries into the kitchen with a change of plans: the meal is to be outside on the Portico top step under the tall columns. 'Can we arrange it?' he asks and hurries away to find a suitable table. I think, at that moment, we would have carried a table and the meal to any corner of the estate we were asked to!

The meal commenced and every time Vic and Bryan came in to the kitchen for the next course I asked, 'Everything all right?'

'Marvellous,' they would reply. 'HRH is serenading Princess Diana with "Moonlight Becomes You".'

The time passed quickly. With the washing-up done and the kitchen tidied, the floor swept and mopped, I say goodnight to Vic, Rose and Bryan and walk along the basement corridor, up the steps and let myself out of the North Door and cross the inner stable yard. I pass the Japanese cannon presented to Lord Mountbatten after World War II. All is quiet under the dark blue sky and I can hear the usual sounds from the river – a mandarin duck quacking and a coot's alarm signal. The owls are hooting in the woods and frogs are croaking in the fountain basin near the anteroom door. I walk slowly to savour all the happiness of this momentous day, blissfully unaware that the guard dogs, unleashed, are roaming the grounds. I look up at the circular windows of the William and Mary stable block where eighteen months ago we had moved into a flat. But it is now the Mountbatten Exhibition Centre and we are in a flat over the garage that often houses Prince Charles's Aston Martin, and the Dove House is next to our bathroom.

Our cat, Perdita, waits for me, having found it is safe to venture out after the excitement of the day. I bend to stroke her and the thought that had been uppermost in my mind in that isolated moment in the kitchen surfaced again. *Just how had I come to be here at this moment – had all those other kitchens where I had enjoyed cooking brought me here to experience the events of today?* Perhaps it would be interesting to recall them from the beginning, because being a cook was never going to be my life – only something that I had always enjoyed from a young age.

One

It is 1930. In a Victorian terraced house in Leeds, near the Hyde Park Picture House, a small girl, aged four, rather skinny, with short dark hair and wearing a long pinafore down to her feet is standing on a kitchen stool. She is gazing very intently into the old-fashioned bread-mixing bowl, enjoying the yeasty aroma and waiting for the magic moment when the bubbles start working through the sprinkling of flour over the warm yeast potion. The bread tins are warming in the hearth by the kitchen fire, the bag of flour is on the table and the long block of Cheshire salt has been scraped to yield its one teaspoon per pound of flour.

I think this must have been the very beginning of my love of cooking. I loved this time in the kitchen; my mother and I often sing together, usually 'Springtime in the Rockies', sometimes 'After the Ball is Over'. She is always ready to laugh and tell me of her first efforts at bread making when newly married and how my father would tease her and say if she gave the bread to ducks on a pond, he was afraid they would sink to the bottom. This some-times leads us to sing, 'Oh Jemima, look at your uncle Jim, he's in the duck pond, learning how to swim.' This kitchen looks out on to a busy road and what we called 'The Parade' – the row of shops so near at hand.

But there has been another kitchen, before the one I am describing now – just one or two streets away in the house where I was born in February 1926 at 3.25 p.m. It was just in time for my sister Mary, aged eleven, and my brother George, aged six, to be greeted by the midwife, standing at the top of the stairs, holding a small bundle in a long white shawl and saying, 'Look what I've got for you – a new baby sister!' This was the time when mystery surrounded birth. Poor things, they had no idea what they were coming home to, but I think they recovered in time! I was to be George's shadow when he played with his friends and I didn't mind being teased when they sang, 'Little Betty Bouncer loved the announcer down at the BBC.' Mary also found she had a shadow when eventually the boyfriends came around, but I was a useful messenger when she couldn't go dancing and had to have an evening in to do some ironing or mend her stockings.

This house was also in a row of terraced houses with a sitting room only to be used at the weekends, but the kitchen was known as a 'kitchen-living room'. It was the hub of the house, from the fire being lit in the range early in the morning. It had a hot-water tank at the side and the water was drawn off by a tap when required, through all the activities of the day. The kitchen was large, square and the scene of all family meals and comings and goings. The large table in the centre was always given its full title – the oak-leaf table – because of the two extra leaves brought into use by feeling underneath for two metal brackets which were drawn across to support the extra panels. Most times the child detailed to this task was rebuked for not lifting the leaf high enough and so drawing the metal across with a rasping noise. The table had sturdy, almost melon-shaped legs and came from the Foster family home in Killinghall Road, Bradford. There was great pleasure in recognising an identical table in the Estate Room of Stanway House, Gloucestershire, in 1989. Tales were told of Father's dog, Badger, being tied to one of the table legs and kept in the kitchen because he was not popular with Grandma Foster (Mary Emily). Between meals, the table, in my time, was covered with a heavy chenille cloth, to be found in most houses. It was wonderful plushy material sometimes in a

13

deep green, but ours was autumn reds, ochres and browns. Such a sturdy material, it lasted for years, though scarred by cigarette burns from carelessly dropped ash or little furrows drawn with a pen while homework worried and teased a child. It provided the perfect texture for my toy farmyard to be set out upon and, in my imagination, it became ploughed fields when toy hedges enclosed the cows and sheep.

Meal times were so punctual and when the cry went up, 'Clear away, set the table,' all had to be abandoned. The sink was an interesting feature or, if required, non-feature of the kitchen. It was a deep white glazed sink with a wooden draining board and it was enclosed within cupboard doors. The small cupboards underneath were, in one half, the shoe cupboard and, in the other half, a toy cupboard. So, the washing up completed, the door could be closed and this aspect of the kitchen forgotten. It then became the living room and a lot of time was spent sitting around the table for, besides the five of the family, for a time there was another Mary – a girl who lived in as Mother's help. There was once a special visit, when she asked to take George and me to her home at Newmillerdam near Wakefield. I have a very early memory of this – walking into a farm kitchen, kneeling on a rag rug and looking into a cardboard box and seeing, to my delight, a mother cat and her new kittens. So it stays with me – the special feeling of knowing this was somewhere different and how much I liked it. Perhaps this was a foretaste of the two farm kitchens I would live in and the railway cottage and the two estate lodges.

The sink behind the doors provided a playtime area for my brother George as a small boy when, on wet weekend afternoons, the usual 'playing out' straight after the meals was not practical. Standing on a kitchen stool, rubber apron tied around his middle, he filled and refilled a selection of bottles with a funnel and jug and declared himself to be selling dandelion and burdock, or possibly beer. So a future career as a publican was prophesied for him, but it was not to be realised – he was destined for the Bradford wool trade.

It was in this kitchen that I was sung to sleep to the strains of Lehár's *The Merry Widow* waltz and it was here that my very favourite and most loved toy was given to me. Various members of the family had been to Woodhouse Moor Feast and someone had won a prize other than the usual coconut. On arriving home, the back door was opened and Old Ted (as he became) was pushed into the room. It was love at first sight! He was not a teddy bear but a toy dog and, in memory, quite large. He was sitting down, front legs outwards, and had a round tail, strange gingery-brown fur and a white front. He looked old and wise from the beginning and was always the leader of the toys. When a smart new teddy came later on, he became Old Ted.

The window of the kitchen looked out on to a small yard where there was a high wooden gate, two small privet hedges and, near the window, a folding garden seat (still to be seen in photographs until 1950). Often to be seen near the seat was a jar of bluebells – a town child's pride and joy, gathered at Lawnswood or on the Ridge – and often a jar of tadpoles or sticklebacks. That was the sum total of nature study.

There were a lot of songs to be remembered from this time and Mother's repertoire was very varied, ranging from 'Seated One Day at the Organ' to 'The Last Rose of Summer', 'The End of a Perfect Day' and music-hall songs, hymns and light opera. I remember my sister, Mary, and brother, George, teaching me: 'Eleven more months and ten more days I'll be out of the calaboose. Eleven more months and ten more days they're going to turn me loose.' I had no idea what a 'calaboose' was and neither did they, but we all sang with great vigour.

Around the time that I was four years old came the move to the next house and a new kitchen. This house was at

2 Hessle Place and was only one street away from the last house. In fact, it was nearer to Wrigglesworth's baker's shop, who sold such delightful iced buns. On the other side of the road was The Parade – a row of shops which provided for every need.

The kitchen at Hessle Place was smaller because now there was a dining room as well as a drawing room. Again there was a fire oven and now I can remember the gas cooker, heavy and old-fashioned (a Main cooker) standing high on its legs; the burners were so cumbersome and heavy. Each burner had to be lifted off and immersed in hot water in which washing soda was dissolved and then they were scrubbed. At this time in the '30s soda was often used in the washing-up water, causing red chapped hands. All soap scraps were saved and placed in a little wire basket with a long handle, which could be swished in the water to make foam. Also there was Monkey Soap – a rather gritty, miserably grey block; it was a cleaner for sinks. Again on the cleaning note, in the corner of this kitchen there was the set pot – so called, I think, because the white clothes to be boiled on Monday washday were placed or 'set' in this deep, cauldron-like container. Underneath it was a small fireplace where a fire was lit early on Monday morning and the clothes were 'set' to boil. The odour of carbolic soap would then hang about the house all day. The work involved stirring the clothes with a poss stick and then rubbing it on a Peggy Board (a ribbed board of the type now used by skiffle country and western players). Then followed starching and the blueing of white clothes. A Dolly Blue Bag was dipped up and down in hot water and the clothes then rinsed in this bright blue water. When they dried, the blue tinge gave the clothes the impression of being ultra white!

Because of all this hot steamy labour there was little time for cooking for the family, who turned up as regular as clockwork for the midday meal. They came from their schools and from their places of work. So Monday lunch was always slices of cold meat from the Sunday joint and bubble and squeak. A rice pudding was also cooked in the fire oven because there was always a fire to heat the water, even on the hottest summer day.

So this kitchen was small, cosy and, from memory, a happy place to play in. On winter evenings the family were ensconced in the dining room and the fire was left to die out, but was still bright enough to gaze into. The fire basket was placed high and had bars you could put the poker through so that with a rattle lots of bright red cinders would cascade into the ashes below – like lava from a volcano. Songs remembered here include 'When it's Springtime in the Rockies', Betty Boop – 'If I Had a Talking Picture of You' and always *The Blue Danube Waltz*, particularly played at Mary's twenty-first party. My best friend Derrick would come round to play and here we rehearsed our concerts to which the family were invited and they paid with a farthing coin. There were usually recitations and then a tableau of a historical nature. We were a little surprised when everyone convulsed with laughter at the sight of Derrick dressed as Queen Victoria. Derrick was a very dark-haired, sallow-skinned boy, but tastefully dressed, I thought, in a shawl and a net curtain draped from the head, but with a ruched effect on top to give the appearance of a crown.

Daytime playing was happy thanks to Mother's imaginative gifts. What a happy thought to have a swing attached to the lintel of the back door, although it can't have been easy to have a child flying backwards and forwards out to the yard and into the kitchen for many an hour.

The swing was bought at Woolworths and at that time every article was 6d or 3d, so the substantial wooden seat was 6d and the ropes 3d each, the hooks also 3d each.

I dreamt so many hours away on that swing. The yard was small and this time there was an iron gate so children could look in and see George's white mice in their cage hanging on the wall. There was a very small patch of soil in the corner, planted with London Pride and Montbretia flowers.

I was always convinced a donkey could be kept here and that it would complete my life!

On 13 September 1994 I took a sentimental journey to 2 Hessle Place with Mary. The most poignant detail of the house was that the two hooks for the swing were still firmly attached to the lintel of the door – sixty-two years later! Good workmanship on the part of Mr Swallow, owner of the ironmonger's shop.

The kitchen window looked on to the high brick wall of the last of the shops in the parade. This was a shoe repairers and the wall was their advertising space. Painted on the brickwork in bold lettering was: 'Express repairing for long wearing. Repairers of fashion shoes.' Reading this just became a part of life, it was the backcloth to all our comings and goings.

When it was dark on a winter's evening and all other lights were out, the gas street lamp outside the yard gate cast a friendly glow into the kitchen. As a small child, usually on the days when I was home from school recovering from illness such as measles or mumps, there was great pleasure to be had in waiting for the lamp to be lit by the lamplighter. He came along with the short ladder, triangular in shape, leaned it against the lamp and lit the gas mantle; thus the evening had begun. As Robert Louis Stevenson said in his poem 'The Lamplighter', 'For we were very lucky with a lamp before the door.' This was one of my husband John's favourite childhood poems.

The furnishing of the kitchen was simple – there was a large chest of drawers painted green. The drawer handles were round, faceted glass and on the top an extra wooden piece had been added to make a working table. It was here that I was introduced to the magic of waiting for the large earthenware bread bowl to be placed before me. Mother weighed out the flour and added salt from a long package wrapped in sturdy paper and marked 'Cheshire salt'. Then came the small bowl and that block of yeast, clammy to the touch, and a smell that even now can evoke the memory of making bread, long ago. One ounce was crumbled into the bowl and a teaspoon of sugar sprinkled over it, a small amount of lukewarm water was added and finally a sprinkling of flour.

I was now the keeper of the yeast – detailed to wait for those bubbles that would mysteriously appear, pushing their way through the covering of flour. It was such a special ritual. Mother, in the meantime, had rubbed in the lard, measured out the water and scooped out a deep well in the flour mixture. When we decided my frothy libation was ready, I was allowed to tip it into the well and was told to clean the bowl out to make sure every last bubble went into the flour. Now came the kneading and the strengthening; finally the bowl was covered with a tea towel and it was set before the fire to rise. We occasionally peeped under the cloth and perhaps, after an hour had passed, there was the dough at the top of the bowl. The same ritual always followed – a light tap and the words: 'Smooth as a baby's bottom.'

There were also the silver-cleaning mornings, when a newspaper was spread over our working area and the silver to be cleaned spread out before us. The teaspoons were mine and much energy went into their polishing. Mother would sing and tell me stories of her childhood, especially about the three cats – Half-Tail, No-Tail and Three Legs. Hers was an unusual childhood; she was adopted by an aunt and uncle when, as the youngest of thirteen children, her mother died at her birth. She was taken to live in a flat over a bank in the centre of Sheffield where her aunt and uncle were caretakers. Her uncle had been in the Indian army and was to die young.

Dear Mother, who could think of such wonderful pastimes! Perhaps my favourite was the salt-pattern game. A whole packet of salt (kept just for me) was emptied on to the table and smoothed out with a rolling pin, like a new canvas prepared for the artist. To one side were a variety of implements – a biscuit cutter, spoons, a fork and a skewer, and I was ready to stamp patterns and draw with the skewer.

A week before Christmas we rose to very artistic heights. First of all came the decorating of the mirror hanging over the dining room mantelpiece. We mixed some whiting in a jam jar and marked out a hilly landscape, a roof with chimneys nestling in the hills, smoke rising from the chimneys, a sprig of holly in one corner and, my contribution, the dots of snow all over the mirror. Finally 'Merry Christmas' was written at the top.

Then we borrowed the round shaving mirror from the bathroom and opened up our small box of Eskimo figures, also purchased from Woolworths and stored away since the previous Christmas. Cotton wool was glued on to the mirror but a circle of glass was left uncovered in the middle and the fishing Eskimos were carefully placed around their pool. Igloos, made from halved eggshells appeared. Then Eskimos on sledges and finally, the best touch of all, we sprinkled glitter over our scene and it was ready to be the centrepiece of the table.

In a far corner of the kitchen was my least favourite door. This was the door that opened to reveal the cellar steps – they felt so gloomy and forbidding, even the cold air that brushed my face was not pleasant. The top of the stone steps (these steps were scrubbed and painted with whiting – a limewash – at spring-cleaning time) was always known as the 'cellar head'. There was enough space to store brooms and the Ewbank carpet sweeper.

George's tasks seemed mostly confined to the cellar, which at times he rather resented, as carrying the coal was the most important of these. Down he went with a large galvanised coal bucket, filled it and, to make his point about the labour involved, would make hard work of returning upstairs, dragging his feet and singing 'Yo ho, heave ho' from 'The Song of the Volga Boatmen'.

Shoe cleaning also took place on the top step. It was considered essential to step out of the house wearing clean shoes – well polished, or whitened if canvas. Woe betide anyone who had made sure they were bedecked with fancy clothes but were wearing dull shoes. Father's voice would be heard saying, 'A shilling head but a farthing tail!' What a telling remark and one which will stay tucked away in my mind for ever, along with all those songs, music-hall ditties and ballads that were the accompaniment to our tasks and play. But perhaps *The Blue Danube Waltz* is the one to bring back that busy kitchen.

1937 and the Fosters were on the move again, leaving behind our familiar shops and their owners, 'Swallows', the undertaker and the ironmonger whose Miss Cheetham would let me stand with her behind the counter, pretending to serve. Mack's newsagent and the Misses Harpers' sweet shop where I saw my first box of Black Magic and thought it was a conjuring outfit. Here Father bought Needler's orange chocolate as the treat for 'In Town Tonight', our Saturday night favourite on the wireless. Only so many squares were given out and these were bitten in two and ranged along the chair arm to be eaten at very regular intervals. There was the butcher whose window display consisted of rows of cardboard cut-out woolly New Zealand lambs. If we asked nicely, sometimes he would give one away, which was a great treasure. There was the Sunshine stores. Then Plaice the barber's shop and Wade's the chemist.

But now it was pastures new, away from Leeds and closer to Bradford for Father to be nearer to Priestley's Ltd and his beloved Wool Exchange. In the past, he had travelled by bus and train. The train left from the station whose Queens Hotel was the meeting place, so long ago in 1910, of George Edward and Dorothy Louise. Dolly, as he called her. She was the manageress of the ladies' café but occasionally took charge of the tobacco kiosk and it was here she sold him some cigars, and from such meetings do our stars enter the firmament.

We come now to a semi-detached modern house, as they were called in the '30s. Built in 1935 and costing £500 each, they boasted a pleasant bay window, leaded lights on the front door and a garden front and back, but they each had such a dreadful kitchen – long and narrow and lacking the cosiness of the coal fire. Despite the appeal of the new house, the kitchen had somehow been overlooked. This was to be our home for three years and then the strangest of removals – from 4 Ederoyd Drive to 6 Ederoyd Drive. Complications had arisen in the renting of No. 4 as it was for sale and cross words had been exchanged. The owner of No. 6, widowed with two young children, was moving out (because the start of the Second World War had been declared) and was pleased for the Fosters to rent her house and later buy it.

No. 6 was to see the wartime years and all its various happenings – blackout curtains, flasks and hot-water bottles prepared for the nights spent in the air-raid shelter. Here my serious cooking began: rationing created the challenge of eking out ingredients and the need for improvisation.

September 1939 came and we had to prepare for the blackout. Yards of green twill material, sent from Priestley's Mill at Laisterdyke (Father was the yarn buyer for Sir Edford Priestley) were made into curtains. There always seemed to be chinks of light showing and the most fool-proof method was to pin the curtains to the woodwork with drawing pins, but very soon these became unobtainable. Wartime cookery books were studied carefully and new ingredients were used ingeniously – dried egg, soya flour, glucose if you had black-market supplies, or a medical note for an invalid. Bottling fruit became of the utmost importance – Camden tablets were added to the bottled apple slices and strange lengths of apple rings threaded on to string were dried in the airing cupboard and eventually looked like wrinkled chamois leather.

Carrots became very important for sweetening cakes and were handed out in scrubbed sticks to any child desperate for sweets. Soya flour flavoured with almond essence could be made into a very passable imitation marzipan. Vinegar combined with baking powder could give a boost to cake mixture when there were few eggs. In the larder, which was in fact the space under the stairs, a bread crock was filled with egg-preserving solution and before winter, if extra eggs were sometimes obtainable, they were put into this rather murky liquid (water glass or isinglass).

At this time, Cadbury's held wartime cookery demonstrations at the Gas showrooms in Bradford and there we gathered to be told new ways of using our rations. I hurried home with the treats and, over fifty years later, I am still using the chocolate biscuit recipe.

There was lots of neighbourly talking in this kitchen; a quick tap on the door and someone would peep in – in fact, hurry in if it was dark, so as not to let out that chink of light that would bring reproof from the ARP wardens. People would call with letters from serving relatives, compare notes and ask if we had heard from George.

FOOD FACTS

Savoury Flan

THE WISE HOUSEWIFE plans her meals to include the vegetables that are plentiful at the moment. Carrots are unusually plentiful just now, and here are some recipes the family will enjoy.

CURRIED CARROTS (FOR 4)

Ingredients: 2 lb. carrots, 8 oz. chopped onion, 4 level teaspoons curry powder, 1 oz. cooking fat *or* dripping, 1 oz. flour, 1½ level teaspoons salt, ¼ level teaspoon pepper, 2 oz. sultanas *or* other dried fruit, 1 level teaspoon chutney. (If no fruit is available use 2 tablespoons chutney.)

Method: Prepare and slice the carrots. Cook in boiling water until tender. Drain well, saving ½ pint water in which they were boiled. Fry the onions and curry powder gently in the fat until the onions are tender but not brown. Work in the flour, add the carrot water and bring to the boil, stirring all the time; boil for 5 minutes. Add the fruit, chutney and seasoning. Pour over the carrots, and serve hot.

CARROT & CHEESE TOAST

Ingredients: 6 oz. finely grated carrot, 2 oz. finely grated cheese, ½-1 level teaspoon dry mustard, 1 oz. margarine, melted, 2 teaspoons vinegar, 4 rounds toast, cut from a large loaf.

Method: Mix the carrot, cheese, mustard, margarine and vinegar together until smooth and creamy. Spread on the toast and brown under the grill or serve cold.

SAVOURY FLAN (FOR 4)

Ingredients: *Pastry:*—2 oz. plain flour, 2 oz. medium oatmeal. ½ level teaspoon salt, ½ level teaspoon baking powder, ½ oz. lard *or* cooking fat, 1 tablespoon water (no more!) *Filling:*—3 medium sized carrots (cooked with vegetables of a previous meal), ½ oz. dripping, 1 medium onion, finely chopped, 1 oz. flour, ½ pint vegetable water (or ½ milk and ½ vegetable water), a little sage *or* parsley if liked, 2 oz. corned beef, seasoning.

Method: Make pastry and roll out to fit a 7" sandwich tin. Ease pastry to fit well into sides and corners, pressing gently but firmly. Neaten edges. Bake at top of hot oven 10 to 15 minutes. Melt dripping in saucepan, add onion and cook gently, add flour and gradually add the liquid and seasoning. Bring to boil and boil 5 minutes. Slice corned beef and arrange in hot pastry case, pour over ½ the sauce, add the sliced carrots and pour over the remaining sauce. Serve hot.

Get Ready NOW for your NEW Ration Book

You may have difficulty in getting your new Ration Book in April *unless* your identity card is right. Look at it now. Is the last address on it the one where you are now living? If not, take your identity card and Ration book at once to your local Food Office to get them put right.

N.B. New Ration Books will be issued much earlier this year—from April 4

THE MINISTRY OF FOOD, LONDON, S.W.1.   FOOD FACTS No. 457

Ministry of Food pamphlets published during the War

At the age of fifteen I was very pleased to be running the local National Savings Movement group and often the kitchen would become the office. If anyone had been out during my weekly call round the neighbourhood, they would ask for a 2/6d stamp or bring 15/- worth of stamps to be converted into a National Savings certificate.

Breakfasts were important, particularly when braving the elements in winter and walking to the bus stop. When waiting in that shivering group it was advisable to be fortified with porridge – not much rationing problem there – or, and this was true bliss, a sausage sandwich. This was Father's culinary masterpiece. The sausages were chipolatas bought in the German pork butchers in Leeds Road. Fried to perfection, the sausages were then split and placed between two slices of fried bread and, with a little care and finesse, dried egg could be mixed and made into a flat pancake when fried in dripping (which added to the flavour). Timing was essential here as a rubbery texture was soon reached.

The kitchen became my province at the age of fourteen. During my mother's illness at that time, I would hurry home from school at lunchtime to prepare a snack and check all was well. Then I dashed back to the tram stop, got off at Stanningley Bottom and then there was a brisk walk up Richardsaw Lane to resume school work. We had a cooked tea at 5.30 p.m., then Father and I would put a tray ready for breakfast the next day and my homework could be tackled.

Weekends were pleasurable cooking times despite the washing hanging overhead on the clothes line or 'creel', as we called it, absorbing all the food aromas.

Father would ask hopefully for apple dumpling and if we had smiled nicely at the butcher and been given some beef suet, this was Sunday's pudding.

Washing facilities were still very basic and laundry was

washed in the deep white glazed sink. But then the Acme Wringing Machine came into our lives, purchased at the Co-op stores in Stanningley. It looked so streamlined and modern compared with the heavy cast-iron wooden-rollered mangle of earlier days. Our new treasure had the added convenience of being a table with a white enamel removable top and the sides were speckly grey enamel. Hidden inside it was the wringer. It all had to be pulled upright; the handle, which had been reversed, was released by undoing a wing nut and a large bowl was placed on a slatted stand to receive the water. The wet washing was folded, sheets proving difficult, but careful folding and high-pressure wringing helped towards easier ironing. Surprising to remember that the wringer was always referred to as the Acme, just as the carpet sweeper was always the Ewbank.

This kitchen was to see the preparation of George's welcome-home meal after his demob in 1945. He had been stationed in Egypt and we had not seen him for almost five years. My speciality was then a raised pork pie, or 'stand pie' in Yorkshire parlance (because the hot-water pastry case was made to stand after being moulded round a suitable jar or basin and then filled with chopped pork). This was the centrepiece along with pickles and red cabbage; I expect a trifle was to follow. This meal was planned for perhaps midday or teatime, but travel at that time was so uncertain as the trains were packed with returning troops. We waited and waited. Mother took up a position by the bay window in the sitting room where she could see the main road and the buses passing. The hours ticked by and there was no message. Evening came; public transport ceased and taxis were at a premium. But all was not lost – there was an excellent volunteer service, a team of civilian drivers who would meet the later trains and deliver to the door the returning soldier, sailor or air force man. Sure enough, just before midnight a car drew up at the end of Ederoyd Drive and our returning soldier was there. The belated meal was eaten amid never-ending chatter.

In 1943 a certain John Louis Thornton had entered the kitchen, passing my sister Mary (carrying a laundry basket full of washing to hang out in the garden) and introductions were made to her future brother-in-law.

Contributions to the outdoor VE party were made in the kitchen and carried out to the group of children. We were quite a close little community as the drive was a cul-de-sac and most couples had come there as newly-weds in 1936, buying their semi-detached for £500. Wartime and a shared air-raid shelter built on spare land near Overend's rhubarb farm had brought us even closer, as had my National Savings visits – blinking my way in from the darkness outside to the firelight and cosiness of sitting rooms and being invited to sit down – had made everyone so well known to me.

From 1942–45 I spent three years at Bradford College of Art and Textile Design, but was still hurrying home to do most of the cooking, which was such a pleasure and there were discoveries to be made all the time. I got recipes from newspapers and magazines; the *Billy Bunter* annual from childhood was covered with the linen from one of George's overseas parcels and the recipes and hints were pasted inside. How I wish I still had that book of cuttings. Yet again, here the make-do-and-mend attitude of wartime came into play, there being a shortage of notebooks and albums of any kind.

From 1945–48 I was freelancing as a textile designer using the sitting room as a workroom and the card table as a worktop, so it was not far to go from the kitchen to the designing and back again. I also made visits to Bradford and Manchester to sell designs.

Father often visited Uncle Joe Atkinson, a distant cousin

who used to say, 'Nay, George, we're not even blood relations, just water relations' (pronounced 'watter').

Uncle Joe was the manager of a small mill in Otley that spun knitting wools and he lived with his family in the mill house. I loved that kitchen – it had a raftered ceiling, a blackleaded fire oven and despite being near the main road it was in the country to me. A high wall enclosed the garden and there was a small orchard. If I was with Father on one of his visits, we would have an excellent knife-and-fork tea round the kitchen table. Then after everyone had gone from the mill and we had completed the washing-up in an identical cupboard-enclosed sink to ours, where the tea towels were washed after each use and hung to dry on an expanding wire clipped to each end of the mantelpiece, then would be my treat of the visit. We would walk through the top floor of the mill in semi-darkness. Bats would be flying out from under the eaves. The wide floorboards smelling of lanolin would creak as we walked along and then we would reach a large sorting table, which had skeins of wool scattered over it. Some were rejects because they were tangled in the winding process and Uncle Joe would say in a very expansive way, 'Now, lass, I know you like knitting. Choose yourself a few of the reject hanks.' What bliss! I remember a scarlet wool with a silvery ply running through. Father and I spent hours patiently unravelling the skeins. He would sit in his armchair, arms outstretched, thumbs upright and make a careful swaying movement as I would wind the wool along and if we had chosen the wrong loose end to start the winding, the tangles became worse. No wool bought since has had the special feeling of Uncle Joe's wool, despite the work involved.

Father's visits in autumn to Otley meant that the Gladstone bag (usually known as the 'kit' bag), which was always carried by him, came back full of cooking apples. And in wartime these were such a treat. Opening the bag was a pleasure because of the rich smell of apples. I'm sure the bag still holds that aroma. Other treasures came home in that bag – extras to the rations, exchanges with friends that perhaps bordered on the black market!

1948 brought for me marriage and the journey away from home to London and to the bedsit kitchens – the first one in Crown Villas, Acton, but it was not for us to use. We were lodgers on a bed, breakfast and evening meal basis. John was at Kennington City and Guilds Art School having been given an Army Education Grant, and most of his evenings were spent at night classes, to make up for the time away – three years spent serving in the army. So I joined Mrs Douglas Alistair and Anne (known as 'Snooky'). It was a tiny kitchen there and I don't think there was much storage space. A table held simple cookery necessities and the only heating was by an old-fashioned Valor paraffin heater, and I'm afraid the lingering smell of the fuel will always be associated with toad-in-the-hole, which was a twice-weekly meal.

Two

Next came the move to our own tiny flat in Adolphus Road, Manor House, near Stoke Newington. This was our first experience of the rapacious post-war landlords who bought the bomb-damaged Victorian houses, quickly patched them up and contrived to make as many flats and bedsitters as possible in one house. Agencies were set up where you were required to pay a registration fee, then queue in the tiny office, approach the counter and ask if there were any addresses still available that day. Then there was the race to find the property and not to be pipped at the post, for there was such a sinking feeling if you saw a couple ahead of you and knew the fare for the bus or tube had been wasted. But we must have made sufficient speed to 34 Adolphus Road because we acquired the rent book (3 guineas per week and this from a £7-per-week army grant) and learned that our landlords were Percy and Vere Chapman, who owned other houses in the area. After the usual 'No pets, no children, no Irish' warning there was added in even stricter tones, 'Don't go to the rent tribunal – others have tried it and wished they hadn't!' As we were so thankful to get the flat, we were sure we wouldn't find it necessary to do this. The only humour to be found in the situation was hearing that their house in Brighton (which surely was a mansion on the proceeds of all these rents) was called 'Perseverance', a neat play on their names.

The flat was on the first floor and it comprised a shared bathroom and lavatory, a small sitting room and small bedroom. The kitchen must have been a broom cupboard with a tiny window; there was an old electric cooker, a small table and a food cupboard with a perforated zinc front. We were at the back of this Victorian house and looked out over the gardens, which were long and narrow and all backed on to each other. The most interesting feature was the back of the Manor House Hotel in the adjoining street. We could see into the dining room and watch people sitting at their tables. It was noisy at Adolphus Road, reminding us of the 'Tenement Symphony', popular at this time. On the top floor we had an ageing musical operatic singer, Miss Rowley, who trilled her scales from morning until night, interspersed with, 'I have never been kissed before, so kiss me once again.' Next door lived a family of Jewish tailors and other members of their family lived in nearby houses. They were seen scurrying along the tops of the garden walls at 7.30 a.m. to reach the family workshop, then the thumping and banging of the flat irons and a continuous family bickering and shouting would start. An aged father was often ejected into the garden in slippers and dressing gown. At the end of the day we felt relief to know that the orders had been met and Lenny was dispatched with bundles to take by tube to the East End and deliver them. Saturday was football day and as we faced in the direction of Highbury; the noise can only be likened to the swell of the roar from the Colosseum. So in this tiny kitchen the most economical cooking of all was practised as there was so little to spend on food. A welcome visitor was Miss Louvain Forster, such a happy smiling face to peer round the door. She was the housekeeper to the various Percy-Vere houses, employed to sweep paths, clean the stairs and collect the rents. Her Geordie accent had her labelled as a foreigner by most of the tenants.

The large flat on the ground floor had two newly married tenants who were rather well known to us all at this time – Seretse and Ruth Khama. Seretse was the chief of the Bamangwato tribe in Bechuana land, now Botswana, and had met Ruth and her sister at a church social for the London Missionary Society. When Ruth and he married, there followed serious political and family troubles; the tribe led by Tshkedi Khama was divided into factions and the Foreign Office was involved. So for weeks press reporters hung about the house to watch and take photographs. When Seretse had returned to Serowe in Botswana, they would run after Ruth, shouting questions. On occasions, I dressed in Ruth's coat with a headscarf on and led them down the main road while she made her escape through the gardens at the back of the house.

In 1949, after a year at No. 34, worrying rumours were passed from tenant to tenant. The Percy-Veres were selling the house at a great profit. The bath in the shared bathroom had shown the weakness of the bomb repairs by crashing through the ceiling of the vestibule and remained hanging on the rafters with its cast-iron feet showing to all who entered the front door. Admittedly, this was brought about by the antics of the amorous young lady next door when she was chased by her Greek boyfriend. Yes – the house was to be sold, but we were offered the garden flat at 43 Queen's Drive, near Blackstock Road, Finsbury Park. The garden flat was a basement bed-cum-sitting room reached by the area steps and a dark passage led to a room whose window was semi-below ground.

The kitchen, sadly, was no more than the end of the corridor boarded across with a very flimsy door (more bomb reclamation) nailed to it. This was very primitive and very dark. One wall was brick and here I learnt that mice climb up and down walls very nimbly! I remember little of the time spent in this kitchen but have fond memories of Penguin biscuits, which were newly in the shops. I am sure they were twice the size of the present biscuit as one with a large cup of coffee made in my brown earthenware coffee cups – a present from George – made a pleasant lunch.

In 1951, the army further education grant came to an end and we returned to Yorkshire on the promise of a teaching post for John at Bradford College of Art. This failed to materialise and so followed the freelance period of making the convex mirrors with baroque decorations, which were fashionable at this time. We also made small flower paintings with decorative frames, and, for the coronation year, busts of Elizabeth and Philip. We spent a short time living at home again and Catherine was born in August 1952. We lived in the front room at No. 6 and apart from the baby bath – galvanised iron with two sturdy handles – propped against the wall and a cot in the bedroom, all was as it had been before I left home.

The day after the Coronation ceremony, 1953, everyone was recovering from street parties and the novelty of watching newly acquired television sets. But we were on the move with our scanty possessions. Catherine and I were to join John, who had been working on a trial basis with a Scottish farmer, Willie Millar, on a farm near Wombwell, South Yorkshire (wages £5 per week, milk and potatoes). Having convinced this dour but kindly man that he could drive a tractor, keep up with the others in hoeing and with difficulty harrow a field, we became the tenants of a tied cottage – 2 Low Laithes Cottages – and entered upon an entirely new life. Douglas, John's brother-in-law, brought what little furniture we had in the back of his Jowett pick-up van and George delivered Catherine and myself in his Austin A40. I remember George singing, 'Up she goes the colour's blue,' on the journey.

2 Low Laithes was a former railway cottage and the bridge over the lane to the farm brought the track so close to the house that passing trains shook the walls and when the kitchen door was open there was only a fence and small embankment between us and the trains. Indeed once a goods truck overturned and we were able to dig up the coal

in the garden from that incident. Hanging washing out had its moments, too. On a very windy day, a dress was whipped out of my hands and blew on to the railway line. A quick dash over the fence, up the slope, look right, look left, up the line, grab the dress and back again. There was the excitement of the royal train passing and waving to the Queen and Prince Philip, not knowing that thirty years hence I would be cooking for Her Majesty at Broadlands' shooting parties.

The timetable of passing trains – the fish train to Leeds market in the early hours, the 10 p.m. train filling the bedroom with bright light as the fireman stoked the fire box – became part of our lives. Well remembered was the night Patrick was born and was just five minutes old when the 10 p.m. passed by.

But I am digressing because here was the first of my real kitchens – only a scullery, but I was seeing it in a different light. It had a country feel; it looked out on to a vegetable garden and there was an apple tree. The old-fashioned sink was under the window; there was a small black-leaded fire grate, a large cupboard and that was all. No gas cooker or electric cooker, just an old gas boiler, for the washing, attached to a solitary gas tap. In the living room was a fire range where the cooking would take place, so a fire had to be lit every day to heat the water as well.

The day after moving in, Catherine and I made the journey to Barnsley, catching the bus at the Fig Tree Inn. On the advice of Doris Kendall, our next-door neighbour, we increased our cooking potential by the purchase, at Woolworths (still in the days of being an emporium), of a gas ring and length of rubber tubing. Standing the ring on top of the gas boiler and connecting the tubing to the gas tap, we could now boil a kettle or heat a pan of milk early in the morning before the fire had started to burn brightly. Coal was certainly not a problem. We were in the heart of a mining community and for 30s we could buy a ton of a miner's free-coal allowance. This meant wheeling a sack barrow up the hill, bagging the coal, which was of the best quality, and semi-running and walking to bring this black treasure to our own coal house.

The kitchen saw an early start, as the farm work began at 7 a.m. The little gas burner was put to good use, boiling the kettle and then it was used for the pan of porridge. Catherine, always an early riser, would be sitting in the high chair leafing through a *Rupert* annual and talking to Blue Ted, a small Chilprufe toy with a very fetching blue hat. In this kitchen I remember using Daz for the first time. It must have been a sunny spring morning because everything fitted in with the fresh-air smell of this new soap powder and its clean blue appearance. We decorated this kitchen with a rather splendid wallpaper; four rolls were to be had cheaply and it had a large green leaf design on a white background. Soon after this decorating we were to leave our railway cottage and with us would be John Patrick, our new arrival. Perhaps Doris Kendall's words were ringing in our ears: 'Easier to flit [move house] than to spring clean!' But, no, this was not the cause, but hope that our luck was turning. John was to work at the art bronze foundry in Canal Road, Bradford where at the age of sixteen he had supervised the casting of the VC plaque, to the memory of Eric Anderson – his first commission. He was to build up a fine art casting department, but alas, Bradford did not seem ready for this, as we were to discover!

We bought a small house in Undercliffe Street by what was known as 'rental purchase': a deposit of £50 and payments of 5s per week. This house, on a steep hill, was known as a 'back-to-back' terrace house. A row of houses faced on to the street and at intervals were passageways to the houses which were literally joined back-to-back. There was a small patch of garden and from the only outside door a flagged path led to the outside lavatory or privy. Steep steps led to the outside door and looking down from them through a grid could be seen the cellar window and near the grid an iron plate set in the wall which, when pulled upwards on a chain, revealed the chute for the coal to be tipped from sacks into the cellar. The one and only door opened into the living room, and the kitchen was almost non-existent! It was called a 'cellar head kitchen' which meant there was a large flagged space for a gas cooker. We moved in during February and freezing-cold weather and Arctic winds seemed to swirl round my ankles while I was cooking. There was always the worry that a small child might disappear down the steps into the darkness below, so a gate was fitted.

At this time we hardly had need of the stone slab mounted on legs in the cellar which in the summer was the keeping place for milk and perishable foods. But there was something rather enjoyable about the contrast of the cellar head and the warmth and firelight of the living room. We were confined to the house for some time as the freezing conditions grew worse and it was impossible to push the pram, plus Catherine holding tightly to the handle, without sliding backwards down the steep hill. What a blessing that it was still the old-fashioned time when the grocer in the local corner shop would deliver the order put through his door by John, on his way to work, once a week. Luckily, during this arctic weather, there was an excellent fish and chip shop in nearby Ripon Street. How prophetic this name was to be, for in six months' time the disappointment of the foundry work and our desire to be in the country again found us on the move to Home Farm Cottage, Newby Hall, Ripon, in August 1955.

This was the beginning of our 'stately home' living and there couldn't have been a greater contrast in surroundings. From a steep hill of back-to-back houses looking down on to the Bradford woollen mills to the eighteenth-century Home Farm set in the parkland of Newby Hall, which was built in 1688. Again we were to live in a farm cottage which was an extension of the farm house. John had already worked here for a week, sleeping on a camp bed in the large empty bedroom which overlooked the garden. Beyond was the paddock and, through the trees of the parkland, we could glimpse the Hall itself, the Adam stable block and the road winding through the park. On the days when the house and garden were open to the public there was always the interest of watching the cars drive into the area in front of the stable where the flower stall would be filled with produce and sold to the public by Major and Mrs Compton.

So on a beautiful August evening three days before Catherine's third birthday and with Patrick just six months old, George's car turned into the spacious farmyard surrounded by mellow pink-brick buildings, plum trees growing against the wall and a large paddock called the 'drying ground' ahead of that. As with Undercliffe Street, the children and I had not seen our new home until the actual moment of moving in.

We stepped though the back door into a stone-flagged scullery. There was a sink and draining board, a very large corner cupboard and a water tank set high on the wall. As there was no bathroom the sink was our handbasin as well, then there was a step up into the kitchen-living room. A small extension had been built on and some stained glass had been used in the windows which added to the pleasantness of sitting at the table and looking up at the park. There was an attractive corner cupboard, one taken from an old building and installed by Fred Warriner, the estate carpenter. Our cooking, as at Low Laithes, was done in the fire oven, the usual farm range which heated the water as well, with a back boiler. We had an electric ring set on a black enamelled base with a low–medium–hot control and, with ingenuity and a little switching about of pans, our cooking could be as varied as required. The fire range – I think it was called 'Ebor' – a neat variation on our previous range called a Yorkist, made a cosy corner to sit near on the rocking chair.

So this was to be our kitchen for seven years. Looking back these were such happy years that the lack of a bathroom (we did have an indoor loo this time!) and few kitchen refinements hardly seemed to matter.

A large tin bath, brought in from one of the outhouses and placed on the rag rug in front of the kitchen fire, provided bath-time comforts and at other times it was easy to have a stand-up wash in the white enamel baby bath. Bath time was always on Friday evenings because the water had heated all day when the fire oven was in use for baking day. Indeed, when evening came, ferocious bubbling noises could be heard from the fire back boiler and we hurried to turn on the hot tap to release the steam. On cold, draughty nights the tall clothes horse, draped with towels, was placed near the bath to keep away cold-air currents. A large wooden clothes horse was an essential piece of kitchen equipment and it is interesting to remember the northern-dialect name for it: 'a winter hedge'. It was used in winter instead of spreading the sheets, etc. on the hedge to bleach in the sunshine. Monday was always washday and woe betide a wet washday, for everything had to be dried around the fire on the clothes horse. A bright and windy spring day brought absolute bliss, when the washing could be pegged out on the clothes line and came in smelling of real fresh air and not Lenor.

Baking day started with the ritual of cleaning out the ashes and soot from the fire oven, and soot there was aplenty. The night before, the soot-cleaning equipment was left on the hearth to remind the reluctant one that this must be tackled. There was a large flue brush with a flexible handle, a small hearth brush whose bristles wore away very rapidly, a small shovel, a fire rake and newspaper to spread on the floor to receive the debris. The small top oven was filled with bundles of neat twigs, which were gathered on walks and dried in the oven and known as 'oven sticks' because it was essential to add them to the fire. If done at the right moment, it made the heat roar under the side oven; they were invaluable for lighting the fire every morning. Damp firewood meant failure to set light to the coal and there was much grumbling and making twists of newspaper to push under the wood, then you would light yet another match and blow until red in the face. So dry sticks were a necessity and even today I find it hard not to gather suitable twigs lying on paths or the small pieces of fallen branches, known to us as 'chunkies', or to do any part of the fire-lighting ritual.

So, early on Friday mornings I rolled up my sleeves and I tackled the ashes and soot. The usual ashes from the previous day's fire were rattled through the bars into the ash pan below. Then the rake was pushed through the small arched opening at the back of the fireplace and the cinders drawn out. The canopy above the fire was lifted off and the soot brushed away from the recess inside. This canopy was part of the mechanism of the fireplace. It closed down this opening and the heat from the fire was directed to the back boiler if the damper handle above the canopy had been drawn forward. This was a knob, often shaped like a hand attached to a rod, and, when pulled, it lifted the damper closing the back of the fireplace and the flames were drawn through to heat the boiler.

Next the damper to the left-hand side of the fire was opened and the rake used to draw out the ashes and soot in the space underneath the side oven from an opening below the oven door. Last, but not least, a plate in the top oven could be lifted and the flue brush used to brush away the soot in the flue at the side of the oven. It was a very deep space from the top of the range to the bottom and often the hand wielding the brush was covered in soot, having disappeared with the handle into the opening. Ashes and soot were bundled up into a newspaper parcel and the fire set alight, which drew through its clean flues with much roaring and promised a hot oven for the day's baking.

Starting with the oven damper only half-open it was possible to keep to a moderate temperature, so biscuits were the first on the list. Then the bread for the week was prepared in a large earthenware bread bowl and set to rise at the side of the hearth covered with a tea towel. Pastry next and the bread proved and shaped and put into the bread tins or on a baking tray shaped like oven cakes or plaits. The delicious smell of baking bread must be the best kitchen aroma of all, followed a close second by ground coffee percolating. A bright coal fire, a batch of baking on the kitchen table and bread rising by the fire make for the happiest of feelings in a farm-cottage kitchen.

After the bread was taken from the oven the damper was closed and the fire damped down a little with slack coal. Now was the time to cook anything requiring long or slow cooking. There was such satisfaction in filling the cake tins and knowing there was bread for the week when the nearest village shop was a mile away – either walking down the Crow-garth, a field which could be very muddy in winter or a little hazardous if the bull, known as Billy, was grazing there, or following the road through the park past the Robert Adam Lodges. Cis Markle's cottage was near the gates and hens and guineafowl strutted in and out of the open front door. This is where Cis, under less than hygienic conditions, made the most golden of rhubarb wine that quickly made you light-headed and so I would walk back up the park on winged feet if I had been lucky enough to be offered a glass.

Once again we had a weekly delivery of groceries from

Moss's, grocers of Ripon. Their Mr Kay collected the order on Tuesday so one had to be very careful to remember all that would be required for the week and the order would be delivered on Friday morning. We led such a quiet life, bicycles being the only means of transport, that this event was always pleasurable. Also, we sometimes heard little snatches of village gossip! A butcher's van called from Boroughbridge, driven by Mr Ramus, soon jokingly called 'Uncle Ramus', and the treat for Catherine and Patrick was to be handed a jelly baby each. They took these, without any squeamishness, from large fingers that were decidedly bloodstained.

Three

1962 offered pastures new! For the third time, I had not seen the cottage until we moved in. We moved to Whittington near Kirby Longsdale in Westmoreland for John to become a butler and leave the farm work, as he had the first signs of arthritis. Whittington was a mock castle complete with a high-turreted tower. It had pseudo-Elizabethan cottages round a cobbled courtyard for the staff, or servants which still seemed to be the appropriate word, as we found ourselves in a time warp. We had only one day out a week and this did not start until lunch was over. The silver was put away in the silver safe and the AI[1] plate cutlery was handed over to Beattie Boughen, who would serve the evening meal. We had every other Sunday off to attend church and the household routine was just as it had been in the '20s. The owner and his wife were in their late eighties and while his mind was crystal clear, his wife could not remember the butler's name because the average time any butler stayed ranged between six weeks and six months. Only a man named Jenkins had stayed the course for two years and so John became Jenkins and soon answered to the call 'Jenkins!' without any difficulty. The butler's wages were £8 per week for a fifty-four-hour week.

I now started doing a little relief cooking on the Cook's, day out. The kitchen was old-fashioned but practical with an Esse cooker, a large wooden table and some cupboards. A flagstoned passage led to the game larder where pheasants

[1] AI – the symbol by which first class vessels are classed in Lloyds' Register of British and Foreign Shipping, hence 'First Class'. Also applied to silver plated cutlery to denote top quality silver plating as opposed to solid silver objects.

were hung for at least a week to be as 'high' as possible. The test of this rottenness was to pull a tail feather from the flesh, which was already turning green!

The beef delivered from the butcher was never thought to be well hung, however dark the meat was, so the piece of sirloin was wrapped in muslin by the mistress of the house and placed at the back of the Esse top to warm gently for a day or two. This encouraged a degree of 'highness' that brought dread to the incumbent of the parish when he was invited to dinner (the living of the church was part of the estate).

My own experience in this kitchen was of a very humble kind. I had to wait in the kitchen from 9 a.m. onwards, until Auntie Amy decided she would like her breakfast. With great disrespect, but much enjoyment, we – the staff – referred to our employers by their Christian names and because their nephew was heir to the estate, we added aunt and uncle, but only when they were well out of earshot. Sometimes I could be waiting up until 11 a.m. and so boredom would set in and my attention would wander; it was tempting to gaze out of the window at the splendid view of the Lune Valley and Ingleborough. But that was fatal because when the bell rang I had to be alert and decide whether I had heard one ring or two. One ring was for a pot of china tea only; two rings meant china tea, toast and a soft-boiled egg, cooked for two and a half minutes and not a second more! When the bell rang, the teapot was warming on the stove, a pan of water was simmering and the mesh toaster was at the ready, because now time was of the essence. It was a long, long walk through the house and up the back stairs. Enough china tea to cover a sixpence was the order and on egg mornings it paid to watch the egg timer with undivided attention. When the tray was ready I started out with trepidation, for Aunt Amy's moods were variable and her memory uncertain. For two years I was always greeted with, 'And who are you? I don't know you! I hope you have boiled my egg correctly.' I stood at the bedside while the silver spoon broke into the shell and as one of my greatest dislikes is runny eggs, I had to look the other way until I heard, 'I suppose it will do.' Then we had a set piece of questioning:

'Are you married?'

'Yes.'

'Children?'

'Two.'

'Girls?'

'No, a girl and a boy.'

'Oh, that's clever, some people have all girls.' This she said with sarcasm because there was no boy to inherit the estate. What a relief to escape from that bedroom with its used handkerchiefs scattered about the floor for the unfortunate Boughen to retrieve and wash.

There were two separate households under the same roof and therefore two kitchens. Because of the strict regime, the staff worked well as a team, bonded by the austere treatment meted out. Our own cottage was mock-Elizabethan with chill draughts and winds whistling through the stone-mullioned windows. Having arrived in September we were to face the severe winter of 1962–63, during which we were frozen in and had to place a small paraffin heater in the loft every night to try to keep the water tank thawed out. Again our own kitchen was a living room with a Yorkist range and a scullery with a sink and an electric cooker. But logs were plentiful and firewood and the coal fire made for cosy evenings until you ventured to the back of the room. After eighteen months we were promoted to living in the North Lodge and here one looked from the kitchen window down the length of the vegetable garden, also to the glasshouse full of camellias and down to the kennels where the gun dogs were housed. As we were situated at the top of the slope it was interesting to gaze out while washing up and see all the comings and goings to the Hall itself.

In April 1965 there was beginning to be a definite shortage of money and Catherine's school uniform saw the last of the savings, so, seeing an advertisement in the *Yorkshire Post* for a cook and butler at Newby Hall, Ripon – where we had spent seven years on the farm – we decided to write. We made tentative enquiries and the day after saw someone draw up outside the Lodge. It was the estate agent, Roy Gregson, from Newby who had known us so well and had been sent by Major Compton to ask us to go for an interview. He would pay for a taxi to bring us over to Newby the following weekend. Now, we really were sure that this was fate telling us what our next move would be.

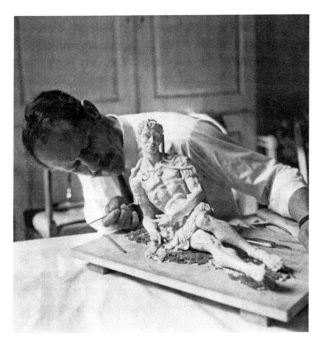

1969: John working on the Centurion
in the staff room at Newby Hall
(between duties as butler and taking guided tours round the hall)

We knew all about the work involved – that John would be head guide on the four days that the Hall was open to the public and care of the antiques would be his responsibility. I would be entering the country-house kitchen full-time. There would be dinner parties and shooting parties lasting for three days. Afternoon tea, ordering the food and being responsible for the bills, bread-making, croissants, jams, chutneys and fruit bottling would be my duties, and everything had to be home-made. There would be busy days plucking and dressing many pheasants. Salmon and venison were sent from the Braemar estate so we were expected to be very self-sufficient. The vegetables came from the kitchen gardens and were brought to the kitchen every day by the head gardener, Wilf Masom, who called at the window early in the morning to ask for the order. Fruit came in abundance; the only tussle was over how much was to be sold on the stall and how much would be allowed to the household, Major Compton being very keen on his sales. Bramble jelly was the favourite jam for afternoon teas and we would gather the blackberries in Braggart Wood on our walks to the river past the derelict Pullman coach. It sat in its own little dell, a relic of Edwardian shooting parties when the luncheon hampers would be carried there from the house. There was still an air of faded grandeur about it, from the pink plush seats to the remains of gilded fittings.

So, taking a deep breath, we plunged into this new life with eleven happy years ahead of us. We still felt we were the art students of early days and often laughed to ourselves when the evening parties of tourists wandered past the kitchen windows and saw us busy with the evening meal. John would be in black jacket, striped trousers, white shirt and bow tie. People would stop to look in at the window as if we couldn't see them and say, 'Look, they [meaning the owners] have a fridge and a cooker and there's a butler and cook.' We often felt like breaking into a song-and-dance routine and dancing past the window singing 'The Waiter and the Porter and the Upstairs Maid'.

Shopping took place twice a week; the order for it was to be left on the long scrubbed table in the middle of the kitchen on Tuesdays and Fridays. This was picked up by the estate driver at 8 a.m. and later in the morning I would hear a shout from the basement below: 'Groceries in the lift!' Opening two cupboard doors in the corner of the kitchen by the Aga revealed the lift and, by hauling on a stout rope, the heavy wooden lift could be brought to the kitchen level revealing the large laundry hamper (a relic of the days when Newby had its own laundry manned by a team of ladies from the village). Now was the time to do a rapid check of the lists in case anything was missing and there was time to catch the driver before his van left the kitchen yard. It was necessary to keep a good rapport with the driver, good marks being given to the cook when she always had the lists ready on time and had sent the lift to the basement with the basket in place to be taken to the van. Catherine and Patrick, our children aged thirteen and eleven at this time, were known to take rides in the lift. A friendly and practical driver would use a little initiative should any item be out of stock and would bring an alternative, or even phone the kitchen from Ripon to ask for further instructions. The phone number of the hall was Ripon 7 in early days, as it was the seventh establishment to install a phone; then it became 007. It had its own exchange in the basement when this area was the 'below stairs' with kitchens, servants' hall, steward room, housekeeper's room, linen, cook's sitting room, butler's sitting room, wine cellars and a beer cellar for the servants who had a daily quota served at breakfast and midday. There were game larders, a plucking room, a boiler room and coke cellars, and a hand-pulled wagon was kept there to bring or rather haul the fuel to the boiler room.

There was also a refrigerator room, with lead-lined

keeping cupboards; ice was brought here from the ice house in the Sugar Hills. It was a little world of its own and so dry and airy despite being below ground and entered by its own front door reached by the area steps leading down under the main front door. From the basement a flight of stairs led to the eighteenth-century dining room, or, first of all, to the serving room for the dishes to be placed on heated dishes. The eighteenth-century stairs were easy to use with a low tread and gentle rise but the Victorian stairs, installed when the dining room was changed to one at the opposite end of the house, were dreadful. They were stone and so steep that one journey with heavy trays would have the legs aching and the breath puffing and blowing.

The kitchen I came to was still referred to as the new kitchen because after the Second World War, Major Compton had quickly adjusted to the fact that the days of thirty servants had gone and everything would have to be more streamlined. The old kitchens were thirty feet from floor to ceiling and the windows gave shafted light from fifteen feet above the floor (to discourage anyone wasting time gazing from windows). So a new floor was constructed halfway up, with windows now reaching from floor to ceiling and bars across from top to bottom.

Because Robert Adam had altered Newby in the 1770s the front door had been placed at the back of the hall and, lo and behold, I looked out from the kitchen on to where the cars drew up for family and visitors to alight and enter the house. Apart from providing interest at all times, while mixing and stirring at the table, it was a good lookout point when important guests were to arrive. Because everything was run so punctually I could time the meals well, knowing exactly how long drinks would last and then the meal could be announced. This vantage point came in useful when HM the Queen Mother came for a visit, when the detective gave me a rundown on the progress of the royal car on his walkie-talkie. 'Now leaving Dishforth aerodrome' meant the vegetables were ready to put in the pan. 'Car passing through Langthorpe' meant whip the cream and assemble the strawberry shortcake. 'Car entering lodge gates' meant prepare the salads and boost the confidence of the helper. Then the car drew up at the front door and Major Compton stepped forward to greet his royal visitor and friend of many years. John was standing nearby to escort Her Majesty and her lady-in-waiting to a room set aside as a powder room. All went well at the meal. Timing was important because the Queen Mother was there to open the exhibition of the replica crown jewels.

There had been a crisis earlier in the morning when the elderly gentleman dressed as a Beefeater found that his tights were wrinkling around his ankles and there had to be some deft work with safety pins on my part.

As always so many other events apart from the cooking take place in a kitchen of this kind, and this was to be so when answering the phone in the adjacent butler's pantry and taking message for WI/Mothers' Union parties asking to book a tea at the Orangery, the café that was used on open days. They had found the hall's phone number instead of the estate office, so it was easier to take down the order. 'Yes, madam, the "A" tea [ham and salad] or the "B" tea [salmon salad] or "C" [sandwiches] or "D" [tea and cakes]?' Then I would hurry through the house to find our house-keeper who, in the afternoons, became the manageress of the café with our cleaning ladies as waitresses (all this after a quick cycle ride home to the village to make lunch for their menfolk.) Most messages were taken first of all in the pantry to shield Major Compton from unwanted calls.

As a family, this kitchen was also ours to use for mealtimes; we had a flat upstairs but I spent a lot of time in the kitchen. I started at 7.30 a.m. for morning tea and breakfast preparation; lunch was at 1 p.m. There was a staff tea break at 10.30 a.m., two hours' break in the afternoon until the 4 p.m. afternoon tea and our own meal at 5 p.m., when Catherine and Patrick returned from school. A short break followed and then the evening meal at 8 p.m. It seemed to make sense that we should eat our own meals there. We soon got used to sitting around a small table near the Aga and being under observation from all who passed through. The boiler man would bring up the mail from the nether regions, and having already sorted it, would hand ours over with cheery remarks on who had sent a postcard. Sometimes he rattled the ashes through and shot the coke in at the top of the Aga and, as this was a very old Aga (moved in from Cherry Tree Farm in the village when the new kitchen was made), we were soon enveloped in a cloud of orange Aga dust.

There were last-minute homework panics for Catherine and Patrick, the usual discussion as to whose turn it was to feed Bun, the pet rabbit. Then there were the times when we looked out of the window to assess the weather and we would hear the heavy sound of their footsteps down the wooden steps into the basement where the bicycles were kept. Our intrepid pair would venture forth for the mile ride down the park to leave the bicycles at the Gallantrees' cottage and catch the 143 York to Ripon bus. Even when we got our first car – a Ford Popular bought from Bernard Gallantree in 1967 – it was only in the worst of weather that our cyclists would be given a lift.

Mrs Compton came to the kitchen twice a week to discuss menus and give details of any visitors and how long they would stay, and whether a breakfast tray would be required. It was always useful to note down in the menu book any dislikes, food allergies or diet requirements of visiting family or guests. Major Compton always laughed and said, 'Never, ever give me prunes or rice pudding' – apparently pet dislikes from nursery days. Mrs Mary

Henderson's favourite was prune mousse and it was more important to Captain Alwyne and Mrs Farquharson to have home-made brown bread, vegetables *al dente* and pearl barley water than complicated menus. One guest had a dread of avocado pears. Major Compton's favourite dish was a dear little woodcock, entrails left in, head remaining on and the long beak skewering the wings to the body, which was to be cooked for a short time in a high oven well basted with a thick piece of bread under the bird to catch the juices. Extra paper serviettes were needed as well as the large linen napkin because the dissecting of this little sacrifice could be messy.

The four days of the week that the house and gardens were open and the bank holidays made for busy times in the kitchen. Lunch was earlier and when this was over there was a dash to wash up, then John would hurry through the house to put up the stands and ropes, open the shutters in the tapestry room and clear away the newspapers in the library, and by this time Major Compton would be on his way to the flower stall. I prepared a tea tray for the guides' tea and left a kettle filled on the Aga and the teapot warming nearby. The first guide to break away from the guided tours (thirty to a group) at teatime hurried through the kitchen, made the tea and carried the tray through to a landing which opened off the dining-room corridor and, while munching tea (two sandwiches, one biscuit per person), it was interesting to hear a fellow guide pass by. Sometimes a curious member of the public at the tail end of the party would dare to open the door and peep through.

Special evening parties were amused to pass down this corridor and realise there was a meal being eaten in the dining room. They didn't realise their learned guide had previously hurried into the dining room, set the entrée dishes on to the plate warmer, hoping to goodness our cat Perdita had not sneaked in ahead of him and hidden herself under the draped, starched table cloth ready to dab at Major Compton's feet as a playful surprise, or, worse still, to lay the length of the plate warmer in bliss! After this, John hurried to the Regency dining room door to guide his group through the house, finishing in his beloved sculpture gallery.

The shooting parties, which started in October, were the busiest times of all and then the house could easily have been back in Edwardian times. Despite the hard work there was always the thrill of seeing the house as it was meant to be – bustling with people, flowers everywhere and the hall full of gun cases, cartridge bags, boots, gumboots and shooting sticks.

Each member of the family and their guests had their own chair or corner of the hall to place their guns, etc. on arrival and all was hustle and bustle. Dogs were taken to the kennels or were allowed into the bedrooms. This sometimes caused problems when anyone tried to enter the bedroom to turn the bed down or lay out evening dress. Certain dogs, one in particular called Nonsense, could turn very possessive in guarding their master's luggage and there could be growling and baring of teeth. Nonsense always carried a pair of his master's shooting socks around the room.

In the kitchen it was expedient to make as much preparation as possible in the few days leading up to a shoot as it really was a case of being on duty from 7 a.m. until midnight with a short break in the afternoon for a well-earned nap.

Guests arrived on Thursday evenings, some to be met at York station, and we always hoped for good weather, particularly in November, so that there were no hold-ups on rail or road which would mean a very late dinner. This dinner was the first of three. Next morning: into the kitchen early and the breakfast list was on the table, which meant you made a quick note of how many ladies' trays were to be set for breakfast in bed. These would be taken upstairs by the housekeeper after the main breakfast had been served in the dining room. Morning tea trays for the men were the duty of the butler and the housekeeper would take trays to ladies-only bedrooms, the butler to the dressing rooms. I would have baked croissants and brioche, which would be put to warm in the bottom oven of the Aga. Next: fresh orange juice to be served in glass jugs, porridge to make and leave warming at the back of the Aga, bacon, sausages, eggs and mushrooms to fry and a large dish of kedgeree. Also scrambled eggs and a constant supply of fresh toast, tea and coffee. Butter pats in those pre-diet-conscious days needed to have been prepared in quantity beforehand. Usually the upstairs trays required boiled eggs, toast, croissants, preserves and a small pot of Earl Grey tea. But sometimes those of a robust nature and build had ordered a full breakfast so then those trays would be to full capacity and, as it was a long journey through the house, all plates and dish covers had to be piping hot and all boiled eggs nestled under a cosy.

All meals were taken promptly and Major Compton was a strict disciplinarian to his guests but more particularly to his family who, if they arrived late for the first dinner night, would look into the kitchen and ask when the next course was due to be taken in. They would make a very discreet entry and try to take their places as quickly as possible.

After breakfast the men assembled in the front hall. Jack Julian, the head keeper, would be in his shoot finery (all keepers were provided with new tweed suits, knicker-bockers and ribbed socks and expected to look very well turned out). Jack Julian would have the numbers of each gun's stand to hand out. Cyril, the chauffeur, would check that all the cartridge cases had been brought in from the cars the night before. Gun dogs would be waiting and then, finally, they moved off. In the kitchen all was bustle to clear the breakfast things and wash up, and there seemed only just enough time to prepare the shoot lunch. This was served in the dining room and followed a time-honoured menu – beef casserole, jacket potatoes, York ham, pork brawn, salads, etc. and home-made bread and fruit cake. The pork brawn was also home-made and when we asked Major Compton for wine to add to this it was almost like getting blood from a stone – the usual remark was, 'It better be damned good brawn if I am giving you my best wine!' The next day would be shin beef or steak and kidney pies. The shooting was such a serious matter and timing was of the essence so guests were not encouraged to linger. Faces were flushed after Pedlar's sloe gin had been drunk.

The timing of this lunch relied on the approach to the house of the shooting party and could vary enormously, so we always kept a lookout from one of the upstairs windows to see when they approached the stand nearest the house. The ladies joined the men for the shooting after lunch. They were inclined to be at a loose end in the morning and would wander to the kitchen with various requests, hopefully not during our short break at 10 a.m. when we ate the leftovers from breakfast and drained the coffee pots dry. Looking back to those days, it is surprising to remember that ground coffee was quite a treat and regarded by we lesser mortals as quite an extravagance.

More washing-up to be done and, as always, the china and silver were washed in the butler's pantry and the cook attended to her own pots and pans. Harry Marsh, our odd-job man, 'pom-pommed' and sang his way through the washing-up with the occasional ominous clatter in the deep sink. We dreaded to hear the phrase, 'Oh, it just came off in my hand!' – sadly often meaning a jug handle.

Now was the time to snatch a short rest. Then onwards to afternoon tea – brown bread, butter, bramble jelly (made from the blackberries in Braggart Wood), cucumber sandwiches, Scotch pancakes and sponge cakes. The return of the guns, keepers and dogs was always a lively, noisy affair. There was the sound of boots being taken off, guns being handed over to be cleaned and everyone hurrying in stockinged feet to the blazing log fire in the library. Jack Julian would come into the kitchen a little later to give us the game list to be carried on a silver salver to the library. This was always the moment where the old animosity between indoor and outdoor staff would surface. Remarks such as, 'Now *you* can go home and put your feet up, we shall be here at midnight,' came from the kitchen staff. Jack would then reply, 'No one knows when we are in the woods at 3 a.m. looking for poachers!'

The kitchen was supplied with grouse and venison from Invercauld and Braemar; the salmon would be sent in plaited fish baskets. Pheasant, partridge, woodcock, hare and rabbit came from the home estate. The butler was expected to cycle down the park to the home farm to collect the milk in two large milk cans. Because of the plentiful supply of game, the time between the shoot weekends was spent plucking and drawing birds and preparing them for the freezer.

The plucking of the birds was carried out by Harry Marsh (Niff-Naff) in one of the basement rooms, which was not his favourite task by any means. Then Annie Marsh (Harry's sister-in-law) and I prepared ourselves for mornings of drawing and trussing many birds. Annie's large hands and swollen fingers – swollen from many years of milking cows – were surprisingly deft. Mine gradually acquired more skill but there was always a slight inward shudder.

Annie's talks of Skelton village helped the time to pass quickly. As she sorted among the entrails and picked out the giblets to be packed in a small bag with each bird, we talked about many aspects of village life. Her favourite topic was the laying out of the newly deceased, so important because she could earn all those extra pennies that over the years had supported her family and, as village gossip would have it, filled a large black stocking hidden under her bed. It was a familiar sight to any of the Skelton folk to look out from a bedroom window on a moonlit night and see Annie hurrying up the street with the laying-out boards under her arm. I was once asked to take a message for her, when Annie was cleaning at the hall, from someone in the village, to give the word that one of the villagers' close relatives had finally drawn her last breath. I think Annie feared the opposition would hurry in and earn the money.

The next riveting subject was the behaviour of various people during the wartime blackout when boredom and opportunity led to many extramarital affairs! It was hard to believe that so many of the middle-aged people I met and knew in Skelton had had such a rip-roaring time in the '40s. There was living proof of certain people's misbehaviour!

Skelton was a village of nicknames, bestowed with good humour on the inhabitants. We knew we were accepted by the village despite our arty background having changed into farming and cooking, when we discovered we were called the 'Thornleys' after a butcher of the same name who, years before, had a small shop in the last house of the village on the Ripon road. Later I earned the name Mrs Hartnell because of my dressmaking and what seemed to the village to be rather an abundance of new clothes.

Dinks Needham was named after a racehorse which brought him the best win ever. The whole village were racing fiends because the string of stables at the hall were let to various trainers and we had the pleasure of seeing the horses ridden to the Tan Gallop in the Sugar Hills. There was a trainer named Bullock, in the early days, whose daughter would ride out and in a very commanding voice shout, 'Hold hard there,' if one of the farm men should drive by on a tractor. The men of the village came to Neville Warriner at the Reading Room on Saturdays to place bets. I once heard 'Ben-Hur' Smith (again the horse and speed allusion) placing his bets over the phone and French names tripped from a tongue that usually only spoke in monosyllables and broad vowels. There was an Arthur Hardcastle who always spoke with his pipe in one corner of his mouth and was called 'Arsher' because of the saliva involved.

The rest of the Needham family, living together in one small cottage, were 'Dad', the eldest and keeper of the purse, Jid, Tot and Jebba. Tot (for Tom) used to work as a length man on road repairs. Violet, always called 'our Bi-let', left to marry Joe Blencoe. Eva returned home from Broom Close farm cottage, where she lived after her marriage, to clean for the boys twice a week. Then there was Beattie, sadly a little mentally disabled, according to the family because she fell into a pond as a child.

Derek Smith, in the village, was 'Quick-shot' because he ran everywhere. Jim Hammond was 'Wally' after the cricketer or, less kindly, 'Chimpy' a man who remembered hiring fairs and who amazed his fellow workers in the hoeing field by taking Beechams powders without liquid, resulting in frothing from the mouth!

There was 'Donks' Leake, 'Melody' Kettlewell, 'Torchy' Wright (projectionist and doorman at the cinema), 'Podge' Robinson, 'Sailor' Brown and many others.

During the last two years at Newby our one weekly day off, always Tuesday, was spent renovating and decorating the small two-up and two-down house we were buying in Harrogate. We were trying to be sensible and look ahead to the future; Major Compton was in his eighties and ill.

Catherine and Patrick were ready to fly the nest and John would return to sculpture and work freelance; I would try different areas of cooking, perhaps also freelancing or catering. Catherine, aged seventeen, was already living in Leeds, soon to live in London. Patrick was going to Hammersmith Art School.

So we were preparing our own little kitchen in Baden Street, cladding the walls with mock pine panels bought at Magnet. We arrived with a picnic each Tuesday and worked until late in the evening. We also made various things in the flat at Newby, my favourite being John's copy of a Habitat pine shelf unit with fretted canopy. The contrast between Newby with our flat in the Adam part of the house and little Baden Street was hard to deal with.

Four

In December 1975 we made the move to Harrogate. Perdita was sedated and John and I were in tears all the way! Irony of all ironies: two or three weeks later there was a knock on the door and the National Trust representative of the area was there saying he had heard we had left Newby and, knowing of John's excellent guiding, wondered if we would be interested in a job at Beningborough Hall, York! But our own house spelled freedom and we were back to the days of being creative. Another of those 'might have beens', but the job did involve a lot of administration.

John filled in with a job at the Rheumatology Hospital in the Valley Gardens and, as he worked in the wards, entertained the patients with tales of Ancient Rome and was a great favourite.

Then came work with Unitex, a fibreglass factory where his modelling talents were put to use creating a hull for the owner's offshore powerboat. Then he worked for Robert Aagaard in Montpellier Parade, restoring eighteenth-century chimney pieces and creating ceiling mouldings and friezes. He got a splendid project at Hutton Sessay for the Head of British Steel – a bathroom with arches of Tritons. Then he was asked to make a copy of this for R Aagaard Esq.!

My advertisement went in the local paper offering an experienced cook to prepare food for dinner parties. An accountant and his wife were the first on the scene – not a very happy experience. But there is one jolly incident to relate. The lady in question, being very lonely, liked to have an audience to see her many new clothes and her collection of a hundred pairs of shoes, so I did once try on a mink coat over my butcher's apron and clogs, plus a mink Cossack hat; I cut a rather strange figure!

Then, at Christmas time, came a letter headed 'Rock Hall, Nidd, Harrogate'. That was fine; it was printed and I could read it. But there followed indecipherable handwriting and heading the signature I could see 'Dr'. That explained all. By holding the letter at various angles and with some guesswork I finally realised Dr Ward and his wife required dinner-party cooking and also cooking for the freezer. Would I contact them before 8 p.m. in the evening as they dined at eight? So I rang and the young man who answered sounded so suave and worldly: 'Yes, Father will speak to you.' By now I saw everyone in my mind's eye in evening dress in a vast manor house. We arranged a meeting at Baden Street the next day. A car drew up, the bell rang and I opened the door to see a very imposing figure standing there. It was Dr Ward, surgeon and member of many committees. He was saying, 'She won't come in, you know. Doesn't know what you will be like!' This, of course, was to be the meeting with Dr Jean Ward (known as Paula to her sons). With some persuasion she entered and we all settled down to a lively conversation. We finally settled upon the following Saturday as our first supper-party evening and so began a lively and informative spell at Rock Hall.

The three boys were all at Harrow. Adam was always known as 'Goofy' to the family and his car, when he acquired one, was the Goof-mobile. Toby was teasing and outspoken. It was he who, in my imagination, had been the suave young man answering the phone, but who in fact wore workmanlike clothes consistent with the stripping down of car engines and farm machinery, and was always working on the vintage de Dion Bouton car in the barn. His hands were covered in oil and rarely changed from this condition. Four-letter words filled the air and were combined with graphic descriptions of operations; this kitchen was to be my liveliest place of work so far. Daniel, the youngest and tallest, joined this group around the Aga on the first night and most subsequent party nights to watch my progress and offer advice.

I was soon known as Mrs B (named after Mrs Bridges in *Upstairs, Downstairs*) and I soon learned to keep a straight face and not to appear shocked. Dr Mark was a great tease and enjoyed a little banter during the cooking; in fact they were all interested in being in the kitchen and Dr Jean would often called out, 'Stop interfering with my cook!' The dogs lived in the kitchen and so we were all stepping over dog baskets. I expected a very high standard of hygiene but was told most things are cooked at 212°F so all germs would be killed. 'For goodness' sake, don't wash the bloody mushrooms – they taste better for a little dirt.'

I used to arrive on my Honda 50 Moped, put it in a barn among the farm machinery and totter into the house to divest myself of my helmet, Peter Storm cagoule, leggings and boots, then don a white apron and my working clogs. Rock Hall had been a barn conversion and the rooms ran consecutively from the back door through to the kitchen, dining room, drawing room and entrance hall with staircase. This caused complications when the main course had been served and I was asked to go to the drawing room to plump up cushions, empty ashtrays and remove dirty glasses. Instead of passing through the dining room, it was suggested I leave by the back door, dart round the side of the house, enter by the front door, complete the various duties and go back the same way. In dry weather this was fine, but wet winter nights were not so pleasant.

If I had prepared some dishes at home, Dr Ward or Dr Jean would call for me at Baden Street. As Dr Ward changed his car frequently and always drove the largest and most powerful models, the neighbours of Baden Street must have wondered at my many departures in strange cars. Dr Jean called often in an open sports car and when we had loaded the baskets in the back she would hand out an operating cap to keep our hair in place and off we roared.

Five

Written in the walled garden, Daylesford, 9 July, 1994

A beautiful afternoon; summer perfection. Blue skies with soft streaky white clouds. A soft breeze, water splashing from the fountain in the small pond and around me an overwhelming abundance of flowers, vegetables and herbs. Asparagus leaves, the smell of catmint, the bronze fennel and the bay trees – this is peace, freedom of soul. This is a coming together of all the beauty I have ever known. It must be kept close and stored away for the winter time.

Meals were substantial at Rock Hall and soon I was asked to appear on a more permanent basis, to cook meals for the freezer and leave a meal prepared for the evening, along with Florentines – Dr Ward's favourites. These had to be hidden as soon as they were cooled and in the tin. Dr Jean and I would think of new hiding places and were once surprised by Dr Ward, who had crept up stealthily to watch us hiding our tin behind the velvet curtains in the dining room.

Operating days brought about a slight tenseness in the morning but great relief upon return. We would all sit together for afternoon tea and I was called upon to chatter and reminisce about cooking days. The gardener would join us and Dr Jean, when in a lively mood, would tease him that she had witnessed his operation for piles, just as later she hurried in to the pre-med room at Harrogate Hospital where I was about to be given a jab for a minor operation. She was not the anaesthetist for the day but I suddenly saw her looking down at me, laughing and saying, 'You do look peculiar.' The boys soon told me never to be ill or expect sympathy in a doctor's house.

My winter journeys on the moped were memorable; high winds meant pushing the Honda along the exposed roads, frost meant a red nose and stiff fingers. But I knew how necessary I was to the household and this kept me going.

Now at this time another part-time job was offered at the former White Hart Hotel. For some time a rheumatology hospital, it was taken over by the NHS as a conference centre and headquarters for seminars. The building was refurbished and new kitchens built, filled with the latest equipment.

Four people were required to run the kitchens on a shift basis – two cooks and two chefs plus waitresses, a kitchen hand and two kitchen porters. I was accepted for the job with Margaret from Pateley Bridge (who was catering-college trained and a little suspicious of my country-house background), George Kendrew, an ex-RAF cook, and Alan, an ex-army cook. We were issued with our uniforms and shown the new kitchens. So much gleaming stainless steel was a little off-putting but we each chose our own work areas and soon proved that designers had never worked in a kitchen! The pastry-making areas were too high and the fluorescent strips shone into our eyes and caused black dots to float across them. So mostly we would find new areas to place our large mixing bowls; the base of a deep sink was usually the correct height. We provided breakfast then soup, salad, sandwich lunches and a three-course meal in the evening.

There was a lot of adverse publicity in the local paper as to the cost to the taxpayer of all this high living and when at the end of each seminar there was a dining-in night, we were warned to keep the curtains of the dining room tightly closed as these windows faced the offices of the *Harrogate Advertiser*. We were convinced the reporters had binoculars.

We worked well as a team. We two female cooks were rather hurt that even when we had been responsible for cooking the sirloins of beef and carving them, anyone coming into the kitchen to give thanks on behalf of the group would always go straight to the man wearing the tall hat and checked trousers. Our white aprons and nurse-style hats did not give us credibility.

We produced scones and cakes for afternoon tea and my pièce de résistance was a Christmas cake for 200 people iced with Christmas scenes and surmounted with a model of a white hart.

One of our greatest problems was deciphering the menu cards given out at the beginning of the week; the choice of courses had to be stated and a signature attached. We frequently made mistakes because the writing was always of the standard found on prescriptions and we made wild guesses!

11 July 1994, 11.15 a.m.

Again I am writing in the walled garden, sitting on the curved stone seat – the thyme seat. I feel overwhelmed by the profusion of scents and colours. The peace is tangible and what have I done to deserve this treasure? I wish I could bring my closest family here to share all of this. I look up to see a bed of feverfew, scarlet and yellow nasturtiums and catmint backed by golden marjoram. Behind me there are rich delphiniums, lupins and roses. The urns in the rose garden are majestic; their goat-head handles are ageless. A wren baby demands attention and another wren tells of a stoat, as it is giving danger signals.

There was good team spirit here and lots of jokes to help the work along. Here I met Dot from Perth, who had been deserted by her husband and desperately needed the work. When she found a small flat we rallied round her with furniture and carpets. We nursed her through shingles and she soon overcame the hurt of the situation and could refer to the errant husband as the 'Outlaw'.

After eighteen months I left and worked for a short time at a residential children's nursery. I was cooking good wholesome food for the children: plenty of cottage pies, milk puddings and steamed sponges. But after this lunch had been served promptly at noon I was then preparing the staff lunches served in a separate dining room and lavish to say the least. A roast joint twice a week and unfortunately for me it had Dickensian overtones of Mr Bumble the beadle and Mrs Corney putting their feet up by the fire and living off the fat of the land. I prepared afternoon tea – scones, cakes and biscuits for the dining room and the nursery nurses took in simple Marmite sandwiches for the children.

My kitchen, which was adequate, was alongside the nursery laundry. This was run by a fearsome lady called Dot Butters, a chain-smoker who worked all day long in a cloud of steam. All the washing was handled here and dried on racks hanging from the ceiling. It was endless as there seemed to be a high proportion of wet beds every night and in winter the drying was a great problem. Her smoker's cough was an accompaniment to my cooking. I enjoyed the children peeping into the kitchen to ask if lunch was ready. It always seemed such a long day and I was so ready to get on the moped and chug along the busy Leeds Road to little Baden Street. We were closed in by noisy neighbours to the extent that Perdita our cat, resident at Newby for so many years, refused to go outside to mix with hoi polloi except for an urgent dash to a patch of soil near the garden shed.

On Saturdays I finished at 1 p.m. This was bliss as I was free of the steam and the steamed puddings until 7.30 a.m. on Monday morning.

Sandwiched between this work was another removal. I had spent lunchtimes investigating houses for sale. Taking the addresses from the *Harrogate Champion* or the estate agents' offices, I would ride on the Honda to all quarters of Harrogate, quickly learning that the estate agents' jargon was totally unreliable. Finally we bought, or rather started another mortgage on, 19 Cold Bath Place (formerly Diamond Place because there had been a diamond-processing establishment there and also a cork factory in the street above). Harrogate being a spa town meant that all its road names related to its heyday in the Edwardian period and Cold Bath Road (which led past Cold Bath Place) was so named because at one time there had been a bathhouse at the top of the road with a cold plunge bath. The Valley Gardens were near to our new house and from our attic window we looked out at the lights of the various small hotels in Valley Road; in the distance were the much grander lights of The Majestic. It was a pleasant walk through the gardens into town and to Montpellier Parade and Betty's Café. There were various well heads in the garden famed for their spring waters. The chalybeate spring was in the town itself, outside the Assembly Rooms, and still worked. From it came the sulphur water that smelled of rotten eggs.

19 Cold Bath Place was a Victorian terrace house and at the back we all shared one long paved area with the old privies and coal houses facing the back door. As Cold Bath Road was in fact a very steep hill, each successive street rose sharply above the one below and the view from the kitchen window was on to the back of the church hall looming high above us. This provided an interesting backdrop and a variety of different music and singing. When we were able to hear clearly, sometimes we caught their Country and Western evenings. Girl Guides and Brownies met there, there were dances on Fridays and after church on Sundays

there was a coffee half hour, at which young children and babies were welcome. Again, as in London, this all had the making of the 'Tenement Symphony' but we were too busy to be disturbed by this. We wallpapered and fitted a vestibule door. John painted the outside and also created a Pompeian niche in the dining room and a frieze of his own casts.

I occasionally iced cakes for special occasions in this kitchen and was working away quite happily on a twenty-first cake when the cry went up from outside, 'The Suthills' house is on fire, it's spreading through the attics!' As this was the house next door but one there was no time to be lost and the cake was abandoned midway through a twirl of icing. After the excitement of the fire and the engine arriving and dealing with the blaze, we stood around discussing the problem, or rather the problem family. This had happened before and the child in question had struck matches in the attic bedroom but, being an accomplished liar, informed us all that a bird had flown over with a lighted match in its claws and dropped it through the attic window.

Life was never dull here. The winters were severe and the moped had to be mollycoddled ready for early starts. But next door was Heinz Priem, an ex-German-army dispatch rider, who still owned a motorbike and sidecar; he would always help. We used to look at this mild, elderly man and conjure up visions of a steely eyed, helmeted, leather-clad German soldier of the '30s, playing his part in the lead-up to the Second World War. Heinz's wife Suzy was Lithuanian and to step into their kitchen was to be suddenly transported to Eastern Europe; there were brightly coloured cloths and lace edgings to all shelves. Their passion and greatest interest in life was caged birds – the house had cages everywhere, along the corridors and in the bathroom, and the attics were converted into aviaries where the birds could fly freely. It was mostly canaries in the attic and whenever John used an electric drill in his studio attic, the shrill noise would bring about a frenzy of singing.

Here at Cold Bath Place we had a fish and chip shop at the end of the row, run by a Chinese family; it was so handy for the impromptu meal. We did notice the younger male members of our family would always be willing to queue for fish and chips, hoping to be served by the attractive young daughter.

The laundrette was nearby and if I worked out my cooking programme I could dash from my kitchen, bundle the washing into the Bendix, return home and dash back to be ready to transfer it to the tumble dryer in the required time. Woe betide me if I was late; there was usually a soggy mass of washing pulled out by the owners and a request to be more prompt next time.

Now for a new adventure and another unusual kitchen and surroundings. I saw in the *Harrogate Newspaper* that Harrogate Council required a cook to take charge of the kitchen at the Lounge Hall and Assembly Rooms (the pump room, where medicinal waters were served in the Edwardian heyday of Harrogate when it was a spa town). This was to prove a job of great variations, catering for many different events and requirements. All of the work took place in a very old-fashioned kitchen, reached through swing doors of stained-glass panels with old-fashioned brass handles, which opened immediately from the café itself.

Everything spoke of the Edwardian age – the decoration, the plasterwork and the circular counter in the centre, which was tiled and where the glasses of sulphur water used to be served. In my day it was used for floral displays brought in by the parks and gardens staff. A small raised platform near the kitchen door was the home to Clarry's grand piano. Clarry Wilson and his quartet provided the musical background to the busy clatter of morning coffee and home-made scones. Another door led to the still room

– the domain of the waitresses ruled over by Edna, who had worked in the assembly rooms for many years. She knew the councillors' favourite foods and all the regular customers by name and she ruled her team of girls with a rod of iron. I realised very quickly she viewed each new cook as a challenge, someone to be broken in to all her unspoken rules, and she could make life very difficult in many little ways. This was a situation that called for tact but also for establishing that a cook was chief in her own kitchen. We did end the best of friends and learned to share the details of all the Council events, which made for smooth running.

Besides the café there were conference rooms, a banqueting hall, a ballroom and, last but not least, the Turkish baths; reached through tiled and marble corridors. They were a very popular establishment in Harrogate. One of our varied outlets of food was to provide light lunches for the towel-wearing, sweaty patrons of these marbled halls. After progressing through the different heats then taking the cold plunge, they were wrapped in towels and then reclined on slatted divans in cubicles in long rows down the Turkish hall. At this point, an order could be placed for poached eggs on toast, beans on toast, rarebit, etc., followed by apple pie. The two attendants gave the orders by opening a small hatch door into the kitchen and as paper would have steamed and become soggy, the orders were shouted very loudly so as to be heard over the noise and chatter in the kitchen. To any stranger walking in this must have looked quite amusing; clad in towels round the nether regions the top half appearing through the hatch gave the appearance of nudity, to which we all seemed totally indifferent. Leftover apple pie portions handed through the hatch to the atten-dants meant free admittance to the baths on ladies' night for some of us in the kitchen. We were a hard-working team, but apart from me everyone was on a part-time basis. The list for the week was pinned up on the board at the beginning of the week after we had all had a conference over a cup of tea and worked out the rota, trying hard to make it flexible for those with families or those with the usual doctor and dentist appointments.

Margaret had been a cook in the Wrens during the war and could cope with large quantities. She could swing the iron racks in and out of the oven with large batches of scones on them, also large tins of apple pie and the favourite, introduced by myself, the spicy sultana tart baked in square tins. Our numbers for lunches or banquets could be up to 200.

Jean, who was very busy at home with a large family and Girl Guide commitments, was a stalwart member of the team. Her daughter, awaiting further employment, came along and stayed, and they had an amusing way of treating each other like strangers while working. Gillian was our Saturday girl, but did evenings too. She was taking her A levels and then going to medical school; it was a joy to see her amid all the noise and clatter – the waitresses shouting their order as they pinned the numbered tickets on a large hook – standing behind a large table with serried rows of trifle dishes, quietly and methodically building up the various ingredients. Everything was portion controlled down to the final rosette of cream topped with a cherry. I remember her pleasure on being shown how to press the piping bag down at the last squeeze so that the rosette shape would appear.

Our Betty C (to distinguish from Betty T) was so full of fun and high spirits, and could raise the mood of the kitchen from chaos and irritation to jollity; she could burst into song at just the right moment. The same age as me, she was brought up on the Allerton estate near Knaresborough and talked of Miss Mary, whom she still visited. She was aware of my country-house cooking experiences and used to announce to the group in teasing tones, 'Now watch, we're really going to learn something special here.' They liked new ideas in garnishing and our salad sandwiches for afternoon events soon earned a high reputation. Little Irish Mary could dart about the kitchen as fast as quicksilver.

We usually numbered six and I do wonder at the amount of food that came out of that kitchen. There was not only the café to be supplied, but the corridors had small rooms that could be hired by groups such as the WI, Mothers' Union and the Harrogate Ladies Lunch Group. The musical festival was held in the lounge hall and we pushed our heated trolleys from one room to another serving soup, chicken and chips, fish and chips, salads, sandwiches, pies and cakes to the aspiring young musicians and their families, to the sound of pianos, violins, cellos and trumpets.

We had a catering officer and I was responsible for making out the lists of food required from the stores and freezers. When these had been approved by the catering officer I would go to the basement where the freezers were located – strangely I had to leave the main building of the lounge hall, walk along the street and re-enter down the basement area steps. There could be no mistakes with these lists as the rather taciturn guardian of the freezers was only on duty at set times and certainly not in the evening – it was essential to estimate to the last bag of chips and scampi for the whole day. Then I had to walk along to the greengrocers to hand in their list. We had ham and roast beef delivered and the bread order had to be seen to be believed.

Three deep fryers were in constant use and high standards applied to the cleaning of them at the end of each day. Changing their oil was everyone's least favourite task and inevitably there was the dreaded day when someone's attention strayed and the used oil being emptied from the fryer, via a small tap, overflowed the container and flooded the floor!

We must all have been cat owners because it was quite amusing at the end of each day to see the row of small parcels lined up at the end of the table full of delicious scraps for the fortunate pets.

Afternoon tea was served in the café and then would follow the evening functions. To my list of helpers I would add three cloakroom helpers, two porters and four bar attendants. Some of the events included the Holiday Fellowship Dance (300 people), the Cromton, Parkinson Dance (300 people in the lounge hall, 150 for the disco) and Burns Night. This was my first experience of dealing with haggis and I was told, 'Whatever you do, don't puncture it with a knife when it is in the water or the contents will leak out!' We prepared bashed neaps and tatties, and I processed with the piper around the room for the ceremonial piping in. There was also the Post Office Dance, the Harrogate Male Voice Choir's evening out, the St David's Day Dinner and many Council meals (following fierce debates regarding the new conference centre).

At the National Dairymen's Dinner I was proud to see Dick the Milk, our own supplier, sitting at the top table. He was Polish and had been in a concentration camp during the war. When he delivered the milk he would call across the kitchen, 'How many today?' If he was not running late he would have a cup of tea and could sometimes be persuaded to sing 'Mack the Knife' for me – always guaranteed to bring a tear to my eye.

We catered for various official lunches, the grandest being the Mayoral lunch, which was complete with the French Mayor from our twin town.

Our most memorable five-day event was the Brewing Technology Conference, in which we catered for 550 representatives of breweries and public houses. During the day some were given packed lunches and toured the area for places of interest with connections to beer and all the local breweries. Those who remained behind attended lectures and slide shows. The beer flowed as samples were being handed out in the most liberal manner possible and this was nearly the undoing of discipline in the kitchen. I began to realise that the large white enamel jugs were missing from the kitchen and were being smuggled back in. The atmosphere was becoming noisier and the laughter level was rising among the students brought in as extras.

Following one jug-bearer I found something akin to a fountain of beer in the Rotunda – a huge porcelain basin where the jug could be dipped in and which was topped up like some giant punchbowl. Despite all this, the lunches went out on time. We were using 30 lb of cheese per day, 70 catering-size tins of apple purée and the sultana sponge recipe read: 14 lb raisins, 5 lb butter, 4 lb margarine, 4 lb sugar, 14 lb flour and 3 dozen eggs. Sometimes we provided food for special events at the Royal Hall – the theatre across the road which in the spa days had been the Winter Gardens and Kursaal.

One night to remember was the Volvo dealers' conference and evening entertainment. Its theme was 'A Mexican Evening' and sombreros were the free gift. There were 300 in the theatre and we were to cook *arroz con pollo*, with alternatives for those not fond of chilli and garlic.

There was a slight complication as the food was to be cooked in the kitchens of the lounge hall and would have to be taken across the road to the theatre, negotiating a busy crossroads at the bottom of Parliament Street and two sets of traffic lights. The food would be in heated containers and stacked on trolleys.

We were ready on time – 21 lb of rice in the containers, the chicken and the Mexican sauce simmering away – and off we went, pushing the heavy trolleys but quite light-headed with the reassurance of being punctual. So we giggled our way across the road, halting at the traffic lights and for those who can remember earlier wireless programmes it was a little like *In Town Tonight* – we halted the roar of London traffic! But in this case it was Harrogate. We reached the bar counter we were to work from and I looked into the theatre at the rows of noisy, hungry Volvo men and thought this would be the end of my cooking days if we ran short of food. My own family had volunteered as extra help and I was so relieved to see them waiting there, looking anxious on my behalf, despite sporting sombreros in true Mexican style.

It was so busy, so hectic, I can hardly remember how it was achieved. But all went well and we were able to relax. I was sitting next to Ken Dodd in one of the stage boxes; he was to give a one-man show. He looked so highly strung waiting to run out on to the stage, but what a change when he started – he joked and ad-libbed for one and a half hours and all of it very blue for the male audience!

Most of the evening events meant we finally washed up and cleaned the kitchen around midnight; taxis were provided by the Council to run us home. We shared whenever possible and again at the end of a successful evening we laughed and joked at the slightest things; in fact a certain hysteria set in and when we alighted at our front doors, neighbours probably thought we had been out on the town.

The next change of employment and yet another kitchen was in order to have daytime work and be at home in the evenings. Also the Head of Catering was hoping I would be prepared to move to the new conference centre if the lounge hall closed down, but this would mean longer hours.

The new job was in a residential nursing home (their fees were quite exorbitant, I thought!). I went for an interview and rang the front door bell; the door opened to reveal a large entrance hall. I was amazed to see what appeared to be acres and acres of tartan carpeting. Queen

Victoria would have been envious of this Balmoral lookalike. The carpet covered the stairs and continued into all the rooms leading from the stairs. But the kitchen was a great disappointment – small, plain and definitely untouched by the tartan madness.

I did not have many glimpses afterwards of the colourful part of the house, just one grand entrance for the interview and then I was directed to a side entrance and a small dark shed to leave the moped in.

The work was reasonable enough as the nurses and helpers prepared breakfast. My task in the morning was to prepare the cooked lunch, which was the main meal of the day, served at 12.30 p.m.

No, it was something intangible that made this a very strange house to work in. There was an atmosphere, a gloom and heaviness that affected us all and perhaps it is not too fanciful to say a certain foreboding was present all the time. Added to this was the perpetual warfare that was carried on between the elderly and wealthy residents, which was strange because most were bedridden and did not leave their rooms. Despite this they always knew if someone had received an extra biscuit or had been allowed a change of menu. I can only think that the nurses through boredom and the effect of the all-pervading gloom assisted in these battles, by dropping the odd hint or passing on some information that had the desired effect of winding up a resident.

There was afternoon tea to be prepared and a light supper set out, then I was free and hurried to the moped, like a bird ready for flight! Our employer was a quick-tempered little lady of forty-five, with two children aged two and three years. Her husband worked away from home and returned at the weekend, when the gloom intensified. One of the young nurses, who liked to chatter and giggle in the kitchen while collecting trays, would nod towards the door and we would know he was listening to our conversation on the tartan side of things, hoping to catch us out gossiping about his wife or the running of the establishment.

I was only there for a few months as I was told of a job at the Home Office Central Promotion Unit, within the Police College near the Squinting Cat pub. This would pay more as it was shift work and would be a little livelier in working conditions. A month after leaving the residential home, the headlines in the *Harrogate Advertiser* read: 'Husband attempts to strangle wife at nursing home'!

The tempo of life altered drastically, especially because of the shift system. Two cooks (female), two chefs (male) plus kitchen assistants and one kitchen porter (Trevor, the tin man) ran a large kitchen providing breakfast, coffee and scones, lunch, tea and a three-course evening meal for 100–150 visiting police officers on monthly seminars and promotional courses. They arrived late Sunday evening, after going home for the weekend after lunch on Friday, and every month there was a dining-in night for 200. The weekends were free and this was such a bonus.

But although the college had emptied at lunchtime there was a price to pay for our freedom at the weekend. We embarked on a cleaning programme that was rigorous to say the least of it and left us all bad-tempered and quarrelsome by the end of the afternoon. We cleaned to Home Office standards and the kitchen was something of a showplace for visiting catering and hygiene experts. We scrubbed, cleaned and disinfected, then boiled water in the vast steamer cauldrons, to swill and scrub floors and wash out the gullies where we flushed away the cooking water all to an immaculate finish. The chill room was emptied and the shelves scrubbed, and there was always the fear of being shut in despite instructions on the use of the emergency handle. What a dreaded thought to be locked away until

6.30 a.m. Monday morning. The sinks gleamed and were polished with a dry cloth and the one action that could almost lead to fisticuffs was to run water into a sink that had just been finished by its cleaner!

And so we wended our way home to the joys of the weekend. The shifts ran from Wednesday to Wednesday, 6.30 a.m. to 2.30 p.m. or 2.30 p.m. to 9.30 p.m. The early shift started with a strong cup of tea made by the waitresses for Des and me, and sometimes toast if the catering officer was late. Then the breakfast preparation started. I had never seen such equipment to fry numerous eggs before. There was a giant stainless-steel pan mounted on a central column that had to be filled each morning with oil and heated to the correct temperature. Forty or fifty eggs were cracked into it and there was great satisfaction to be had in basting and turning them, over-easy fashion, then taking them out at just the right moment with the correct opaque look. Meanwhile the bacon was being grilled, mushrooms, sausages and black pudding fried and also the fried bread was in the pan; that was our pièce de résistance. The toast would be popping out of the catering Dualit toasters and suddenly the orders would come from the waitresses. The art was not to run out of food – we were very portion-controlled by our ex-army catering officer so there had to be no excesses, but enough leftovers for our own breakfasts, which were eagerly awaited until 8.30 a.m.! Never have bacon and egg tasted so good.

After clearing away the breakfast cooking utensils, including draining the oil from the egg fryer into a container and leaving that piece of equipment spotless, we turned to the lunches or the scones if it was your turn that day. The menus were always pinned up on the board for the week. Frozen food had to be taken from the freezers at the correct time – woe betide if you were late in doing this. Our soups were excellent, prepared from stock taken from the large pan simmering on the gas cooker; everything was used in a careful and economical fashion. Apple pies were made by the dozen and steamed puddings prepared in long metal containers. The lids were then clipped on and they were placed in rows inside the steamer cabinets. Our kitchen assistants prepared salads and there would be time to make cakes and biscuits, but through all this we were aware of the police presence as new recruits from Dishforth came to the CPU to use the facilities – mainly the parade ground and the swimming pool. So our mixing, stirring, beating, rolling and frying was often accompanied by mock arrests being enacted outside the windows, the recruits playing the part of the criminal and the arresting PC. The language was colourful and quite upsetting at times.

On Friday afternoon, before most people went home for the weekend, the suitcase men visited the kitchens. These were recruits selling seconds. There was the gold-chain man, the knicker man, the watch man and the shirt man. It all had the feel of market trading! The dining-in night was the hardest work of all, especially if it was your early shift week as you were required to work through until 10 p.m. with only an hour's break in the afternoon. This really was the 'Longest Day'.

The dining-in was done with great formality and equally great expense; the director of the college and his wife were given the deference usually accorded to royalty. We would watch the clapping-in ceremony (all guests stood to clap as the director and his wife walked the length of the hall) and then the waitresses were at the ready to dash from kitchen to dining room. The adrenalin ran high, there was snapping and snarling until the main course was in and then we relaxed. There was lots of backchat as we ranged out the glasses and dishes for pudding and set to work serving out fruit or mousse or wielding the ice-cream scoop across rows and rows of dishes. Then the cheese, biscuits and coffee were prepared and at last we could have some refreshment. We worked well as a team and it was all hands to the Hobart, the dish-washing machine. This was a huge stainless-steel cabinet giving off tremendous heat and clouds of steam; the dishes were fed in at one end and like a car wash they passed through various processes on a moving belt and we waited at the exit to polish and stack. The quicker we worked, the sooner the floors could be washed, the rubbish taken out to the bins and we could disappear through the back door to find our transport. My lift home was with my opposite number, Des, the chef, pigeon fancier and driver of a Skoda. The car would draw up at the end of Cold Bath Place and even the fish and chip shop would be closed, but at last the day was over. Morning shift meant rising early but if you were on afternoon shift, what bliss, you could stay in bed!

Six

Written in the walled garden, Daylesford, 9 July, 1994

In August 1979 came the news of Lord Louis Mountbatten's assassination. Broadlands was shown on TV and I watched, little realising that very soon that would be my next kitchen – tucked away in the basement, reached by a door flanked with cannons and approached down a corridor decorated with wooden shields, bearing the names and emblems of ships of the Royal Navy. On the opposite side of the corridor were the offices which dealt with the opening of the house to the public and the staff whose lot it was to be tantalised by the wafts of bacon frying, soup simmering, meat roasting and fish grilling, all through the day. Any leftovers, particularly apple pie, were received by them with smiles and gratitude.

But there was to be interviewing and organising before the move to Hampshire. We were restless to return to the country and estate life. Mrs Lines' Agency, whose Trudi Hurst never ceased to wonder at John's likeness to Tony (father of Francesca) Annis, sent details of two cooks required. The interviews for both positions were on the same day. One at Broadlands and one at Bleak House, Slindon, near Bognor Regis. The latter was owned by a Douglas Ford Hamill, ex-naval attaché from Paris and his wife. The cottage offered dated from 1791 and looked to the sea.

The Broadlands interview came first at 9.15 a.m. The instructions said ring the bell in the yard by the Japanese gun. We had travelled to Farnham the day before to stay with Catherine, Robin and Lucy. Frosty weather and fog threatened, but we arrived on time and the interview took place in the drawing room, early, because it was a shoot day. We were quizzed at the back door by Eric, called by the butler's children 'the Green Giant' because of his height and the clothes he wore for his work as the gardener. We were shown to the morning room by Ken Stronach, then footman (later to hit the headlines for spilling the beans about working for Prince Charles) and met Penelope Romsey – newly married, looking slim, attractive, vulnerable, wearing shooting breeches, orange ribbed socks and with fair hair à la 'Alice in Wonderland'. It was hard to concentrate on details as the view of the River Test was so beautiful. We left knowing the job would be offered after seeing Lord Romsey on his return from filming.

Onwards to Bleak House, with a slight hiccough because we had to turn back to recover my purse, which had fallen out of my pocket in the morning room. I felt embarrassed to ring the door bell once the North Door had closed upon us. Also I had forgotten to ask to use the bathroom so when a stop was made on the Portsmouth Road at a small pub I had to sprint straight through the building to the Ladies' at the back.

We saw a Slindon signpost at last, close to National Trust woodlands, then came to a very old village and Bleak House itself, which rather lived up to its name. Mrs Ford Hamill was rather forbidding. She spoke of not caring to see anyone first thing in the morning and had a little kitchen, on the first landing amid Oriental furniture, where she prepared her own breakfast. In fact, there was so little mention of food or entertaining that the suspicion began to grow that it was more a general dogsbody required than one skilled in cooking. This was confirmed when a small lady of German origin, working on a temporary basis from the agency, showed me around and when we reached the privacy of the kitchen she closed the door and whispered, 'Do not come here. This is not for you!' As I was already thinking along these lines it was reassuring to have it confirmed. John, meanwhile, was becoming great friends with Mr Ford Hamill, who could see hours of happy conversation for the two of them out in the garden, looking to the lights of Bognor Regis.

We went back to Alma Lane, Farnham, driving past Petworth and were thankful to reach tea, buttered crumpets and a welcoming family.

It was home to Harrogate the next day and a 6.30 a.m. start on Monday morning, knowing that plans were laid for the move to the next kitchen. There was a second interview at Broadlands; Lord Romsey asked that I should not use too much grease in my cooking. We were shown the flat in the William Mary stable block. Our kitchen had circular windows looking down into the stable yard and across to the walled garden, where there was also a dovecote in the centre. The doves were brought from Hesse Castle in Germany, home of the Battenburgs. They had feathered legs which gave them the appearance of wearing floppy slippers. They were much admired by the Queen and although pairs were often sent to Sandringham there was never any success in their becoming royal-slippered birds. Our kitchen window also looked down upon the mounting block where Her Majesty and Lord Mountbatten used to approach the waiting grooms and horses. In early summer the walls of the stable were covered with wisteria and figs.

So notice was given at the police college, the house was advertised for sale and John had to hurry with the modelling of a large section of strapwork ceiling. This was still on the table as the removal men came for our furniture the evening before. Many things were very last minute: one of the waitresses, who was buying bedroom furniture from us, failed to arrive on time and the furniture was left behind on the pavement. Perdy, the cat, was once again sedated and we were on the road to Farnham. Perdy recovered on arrival sufficiently to take up position under Lucy's high chair and wait for scraps of fish to be dropped. Onwards to Broadlands the next morning, in time to meet the removal men. Lots of tea chests were stacked outside the stables and sadly John's stone-carving tools were taken by a light-fingered member of the outdoor staff! In the evening we walked down the park, through the large gates, across the road and there we were in Romsey. We had a meal at the hostelry in the square and made a phone call to family to say we had arrived safely and then began three years of interesting but very hard work.

Because of the assassination, the household was very disturbed; it was a time of change and new routines. Most of the elderly staff were retiring and as a newly married couple Lord and Lady Romsey were gradually altering the domestic routine to suit their requirements. It was almost a year before it all began to settle down. One was so aware of Lord Mountbatten; his staff would be quick to say, 'His Lordship wouldn't allow such a thing to take place' or 'His Lordship would have come into the kitchen to show you how to cook Wherwell eggs' or 'He would ask for a tin of sardines and the tin opener to be sent to the dining room'. Apparently he was a founding member of the Marie-Elisabeth Sardine Appreciation Society and the sardines were best savoured when eaten from the tin.

The kitchen was antiquated to say the least and draughty! There were glass-roofed areas overhead where the courtyard of the original house had been filled in. Lord Mountbatten had installed many naval-type refinements in the kitchen, which at the time were looked upon as very modern. Such as the heating system based upon ships' boilers and an air-conditioning system which seemed to disperse all cooking smells throughout the upper rooms. Onions were disliked most of all. But in reverse when baths were being taken, Penhaligon's rose geranium perfume would come wafting through the kitchen. With great similarity to the bridge of a ship and being below in the boiler rooms was the communication system. This was necessary because the butler's pantry was above the kitchen and accessible either by lift (not encouraged) or by a steep flight of stairs. The old rules were still in use whereby the butler did not enter the cook's domain but received the food from a hatch, or in this case from a trolley wheeled into the lift and then the announcement was made via the speaker in the kitchen to say that food was on the way. This was fine when all was amicable between butler and cook, but at times of stress the two-way system had messages crackling through that were far from polite. George Daybourne, due to retire and whose feet were always hurting, would shout through the system late in the evening, 'Are you still making bloody jam down there? I'm waiting to lock up and go home!' This often happened because of the vast amounts of produce brought in. After preparing the fruit and cooking the meals, it was always late evening when the jars were being filled. These messages were fine when kept between the two of us but somewhere the system had not been perfected and these interchanges could be heard through the house. If the switches had not been turned off after use, all conversation in the kitchen could be heard!

It was a long narrow kitchen and to save space there were sliding doors at the end leading to the lift, which was rather unnerving as members of the family would push them back with a flourish and step into the kitchen. Lady Brabourne used them for her 'Parthian shot' exit. After an amiable conversation, I was told, she would save any criticism for the moment of departure and you would be unable to justify any action or make an excuse. Despite its rather cellar-like appearance the kitchen had two long scrubbed tables which I had always liked having in a kitchen and so I could work well in there. Best of all there was a very large gas cooker; goodness knows when it had first been installed. It had perhaps come from an old London hotel, but, second to an Aga, it was a joy to use. When there was promise of modernising the kitchen I pleaded for it to remain. The modernising turned into redecorating and the installation of a shallow sink, as I nearly disappeared head first into the deep, trough-like sinks in a dark corner.

The freezers were in a corridor, quite a walk from the kitchen, but as all these corridors were lined with photographs of the Burma campaign and enlarged copies of newspaper photographs, it was quite an interesting walk. One in particular always made me smile as there was the double of one of the characters from *It Ain't Half Hot, Mum* in it (Gloria, aka Melvyn Hayes). Down this corridor was the archive room, the silver safe and the cupboards containing the dinner services. Finally, there was the staff room, whose semi-basement windows looked up to the lawn leading to the River Test and on open days the legs and feet of the public could be observed. All visiting staff took their meals in this room – detectives, valets, dressers, maids, chauffeurs, etc. Meals were made in the kitchen and then taken by trolley elsewhere, and at times the thought crossed my mind that upstairs was less demanding than downstairs, particularly when the Buckingham Palace staff were asking, 'Is it G and T time yet?'

Gradually the kitchen became a friendlier place, with a few posters on the wall and a noticeboard with some cartoons relevant to the daily routine. A former secretary (ex-navy) would call in and reminisce of his time with Lord Mountbatten, when he would hold a Monday morning 'surgery' in his room near the kitchen and would hear all the upsets of the weekend from rather highly strung ex-palace staff who had been passed on to Lord Mountbatten!

One person in particular was in tears every Monday and, strangely, I was to meet him again some years later and he was still as highly strung. George Ivan Daybourne gradually broke the rule of not coming down to the kitchen and would sit at the table at the far end of the kitchen and tell me of his days as a butcher's boy in Bridport. When he got a little older, he had been mistaken for a local fisherman, (being bearded and wearing a naval sweater) and would pose for visiting artists.

His second wife was Mafalda, a Neapolitan lady, much younger than himself. She had come to Broadlands because an older brother had been a POW on the farm and stayed after the war, when his family gradually joined him. All staff were given a small vegetable garden and Mafalda, with a little help from George, astonished us all with what could be grown with careful planning and a tiny greenhouse. They grew the garlic necessary for the salami they made and they used bacon bits bought cheaply from Carrefour. The salami was dried out in the airing cupboard and the smell of garlic hung about George's person and breath so much so that the office manager refused to be in the lift with him. They made their own wine, buying grapes at the docks and using grappa. John was once invited into the garage flat at lunchtime and emerged in the late afternoon supported by George Daybourne, who had forgotten to put his shoes on, and together they staggered across the cobbled yard. John was posted in at the door of the flat and for the next twenty-four hours was comatose.

Soon after we moved into the stable flat we were asked to move across the stable yard to the flat vacated by Ken Stronach, who was leaving to become Prince Charles's valet. The stable block was to become the exhibition room for Lord Mountbatten's exhibition of photographs, documents, letters, uniforms, medals and weapons, etc. So we moved our belongings once again and this time my own kitchen looked down into the café yard and, as the numbers increased when the exhibition, as well as the house, was open to the public, our afternoons had a background of endless chatter from the queue below, wending its way in to the café. Fascinating snippets of conversation could be heard, also the cigarette smoke wafted in through the windows. On the outside of the building between our kitchen and bathroom was the old pigeon loft and some of the doves still nested in here, so, while taking a bath, the cooing of the birds through the thin partition was a relaxing sound and, as someone's choice of wallpaper had been palms and a tropical scene, it was easy to be transported to far-off climes. The garage below housed the royal cars on occasion and the workroom entrance leading to our flat became a studio for John.

When John's commission to renew the seventeenth-century ceiling of the Friends Meeting House at Ringwood necessitated working on a shell of plaster, designed to be bolted back into place on the original ceiling with the new swags of flowers cast and fitted on to copper stems, the garage doors were opened wide and the work laid out on the floor. This attracted sightseers on their way to the house and at one stage the Prime Minister of New Zealand's wife found it more interesting to watch this work than to be in the house.

Days were very varied; not only was there breakfast, lunch, afternoon tea and dinner but many extra functions connected with Lord Mountbatten's World College and many other interests. Every year we gave the Burma Star veterans a tea party. The Romseys were called upon for many functions – openings of all kinds including garden fetes, galleries, old people's homes, musical evenings. Also the business lunches brought together all heads of departments and were usually held in the anteroom. There was an amusing incident when, on a summer's day, the large round table was carried outside but everyone had forgotten that the ground was still wet. After the meal was well under way, it was suddenly realised that the legs were sinking into the ground and there was a forty-five-degree list to starboard!

Because of Lord Mountbatten's interest in the film world and Lord Brabourne and Lord Romsey producing films, we had many visiting film stars who often called into the kitchen. Lord Mountbatten had always enjoyed inviting his guests to the cinema within the house and he was sent the latest films from London. The invitations also extended to the staff, perhaps to give the feeling of it being a full house. This was very interesting but also rather difficult. Firstly, we had to hurry the end of the meal and then persuade the person washing up to work flat out, because we were obliged to be in our places in the front rows before visiting royalty entered the room, ready to bow and courtesy as the group entered through the door in the oak panelling of the Jacobean room. Secondly, there was the very real worry of falling asleep during the film. This was more than likely to happen as it had always been a long, busy day and the warmth of the room and the plushy cinema seats soon brought about sleep. George the butler always asked the person sitting next to him to give him a sharp jab in the ribs as soon as his head started nodding, as he would snore loudly. Knowing the Queen was sitting immediately behind usually had the required effect of keeping sleep at bay. This also added another problem: that of not knowing when to laugh out loud at certain points in the film. However, the bluer the film, the more guffaws from the back row. A James Caan film, with four-letter words more than usual, brought forth the royal comment, 'I can't tell a word that man is saying!' Prince Philip then proceeded to interpret. *The Blue Lagoon* had King Constantine guffawing all the way through at the naivety of the love scenes. *The Elephant Man* had the audience slightly worried as to how unpleasant it might all become. My helper Doris, not used to films at all, wondered if she might be excused if it made her feel faint! Eric, the gardener, was the projectionist and it was not unknown for Lord Romsey to stop the film if voice and lip movements became unacceptably out of sync.

We always hoped that all would run smoothly and we would finish before midnight, as with an early start for morning trays it made it difficult to get up. Guests could be late in finding their way to the cinema. Lady Pamela took her dogs out after one dinner and someone was sent out in the November fog to search for her. On another occasion the Duke and Duchess of Kent had been to a lifeboat launch at Lynmouth, were late arriving and brought to the kitchen two very large live lobsters. These had to be imprisoned in the largest fish kettle with weights on the lid and all through the film I kept picturing them out on the kitchen floor.

The kitchen was a hive of activity. There was so much garden produce to deal with – artichokes were in plentiful supply and as there were two ancient mulberry trees planted by James I and one planted by HM the Queen, we would suddenly have a surfeit of mulberries. So rich and succulent mulberry ice cream became a great favourite and was christened the 300-year-old ice cream (because of the date they were planted by James) by the Duchess of Kent.

Redcurrants were brought in large galvanised bath containers and were frozen to use in the rote grütze recipe; this had been handed down in the family from the Hesse kitchens. Also frosted redcurrants became favourites of Princess Diana.

As the office staff increased on the other side of the corridor, the kitchen door would open at one side and someone would take a short cut across the far end of the kitchen and out through the sliding door, looking longingly at baking laid out on the table. The milkman left the crates of milk on a large shelf in the corridor, then opened the hatch to shout 'Milk!' and ask for the next day's order. A fellow Yorkshire man, we would reminisce together of Saltaire and the Shipley Glen railway.

Lots of old recipes were used and some were introduced by Lord Mountbatten to the kitchen – Wherwell eggs, Sacha soup and the well-known lemon refresher. This was supposedly a secret recipe, grudgingly passed on to the palace by Broadlands and supplies were always taken on travels, but gradually the secret leaked out.

At this time we had a great turnover of staff. The older members were retiring and a new butler was recruited, newly retired from the navy. Housekeepers came and went, some in a rather temperamental fashion. One busy morning at a shoot, when breakfast trays were ready to be taken upstairs to the guests, the housekeeper, who should have been ready to do this, was later found wandering in Romsey in a slightly bemused fashion.

It was interesting to find old recipe books in odd corners, particularly to discover that in the Hesse days the chef had previously been a lion tamer! Lady Patricia Mountbatten, now Countess Mountbatten, told of her mother, Lady Edwina, who as a young bride, decided that she must make economies. So when discussing menus with the French chef, she announced that instead of a new fruit cake being made every day to serve at the end of lunch, as had been the fashion since Edwardian times, she would have the same cake served each day until it was finished. He raised his hands in horror! This was unheard of – it must be an uncut cake each day. She persisted, but he registered his disapproval by writing on the next day's menu card '*Gateau Hier*' (yesterday's cake).

Christmas was a busy time here as all the Brabourne family came to stay for a week and only by calling upon my own family as volunteers could I hope to have any Christmas of my own. There was a midnight carol service in Romsey Abbey and supper was laid for the family's return. The Christmas cake featured at this supper; it was very large and decorated with painted panels of icing and one year with the appropriate number of Christmas stockings and names painted on the top. Mince pies were eaten in quantity and soup was always a great favourite.

Nicholas Knatchbull, firstborn of Lord and Lady Romsey and godson of Prince Charles, was born in 1981, the year of the royal wedding. His christening tea brought together many members of the family, including the Prince and Princess of Wales, as Prince Charles was one of the godfathers. He and Princess Diana had just been on a tour of Wales. Sadly it had rained and the jaunty feather in the Princess's hat of plum-coloured velvet, matching the suit, was rather drooping. Prince Charles, while chatting in the kitchen, confided that HRH was pregnant and so not feeling too well. I was called into the salon to cut the cake and had the opportunity to meet Mary Delamere, Lady Edwina's sister and one of the *White Mischief* set. She chain-smoked with great gusto.

With a new baby there was a nursery tray to be prepared for the nanny's meal, half an hour before the dining-room serving. Two rings on the bell meant the tray was ready and nanny would appear from the lift to collect her tray and perhaps remind me, 'A little more cream, please.' She would return from her day off during the evening, but on one occasion, when Lord and Lady Romsey were due to open a local art exhibition, her train had been delayed and Nicholas was brought to the kitchen in his carrycot, for me to look after during the dinner preparation.

In the summer of 1980, as the kitchen had settled into a steady routine for the new household of Lord and Lady Romsey, there came an awareness that Prince Charles was visiting more frequently at the weekends. We were used to the polo weekends, when I could hear the arrival of detectives and the valet, and the lift would be filled with luggage. On one occasion the wrong button was pressed and the lift descended to the basement. The doors opened automatically to reveal brightly polished polo boots, standing amid polo equipment and luggage. No one was in the lift; the luggage was meant to be on its way up to the bedroom. As I gazed from my kitchen table, I remember thinking that in my textile-designing days I could not have thought of myself preparing for a royal weekend at Broadlands and seeing the royal luggage.

How strange it seems to be writing this in the week that the divorce of Charles and Diana has been finalised. But sixteen years ago the story was just unfolding and, in my kitchen, I was to be a small part of the weekends before the engagement. Running up the short flight of stairs from the kitchen to the butler's pantry one day, I became aware of a shy-looking figure, standing alone in the pantry. My first impression was of her dark blue eyes and long eyelashes, short hair, bright blue sweater with two cerise stripes across the front and a white frilled collar worn turned up – soon to be copied as a new fashion. We smiled and that was my first glimpse of Lady Diana Spencer. She soon became a familiar presence in the kitchen – sitting on the high stool, enjoying a glass of milk, perhaps an apple turnover and frosted redcurrants, when the currants were in season. As the months passed by, the publicity and speculation increased, but we all grew used to the regular visits and respected their privacy.

I would sometimes cook at Royal Avenue, the Romseys' London house. The kitchen opened immediately into the dining room making supper parties very intimate affairs, the cook being in close contact. There was an evening in February 1981 when Prince Charles came to discuss events, when he was about to leave for Australia, 'Not on holiday as some people will have it.' I happily clattered dishes and pan lids in an effort not to be listening. When coffee was served in the drawing room upstairs I prepared a meal for John Maclean, the detective, and waited for Patrick and Sue, my son and daughter-in-law, to ring the front door bell to take me back to stay the night at Medfield Street. They stepped into the hall quite prepared to see Prince Charles descend the stairs at any moment. We drove away from what had been a busy evening and one full of portents of an imminent announcement.

It was also a busy time for charity affairs on behalf of Lord Mountbatten's World Colleges, etc. The new butler had replaced George Daybourne and together we drove from Broadlands in the Range Rover loaded with plates, knives, forks, silver, linen and food to prepare for an evening buffet at Royal Avenue hosted by the Romseys for the Royal College of Nursing. Such a busy day to prepare the house, which entailed going up and down between three floors. My centrepiece for the table, instead of flowers, was a large arrangement of vegetables. Onions were cut across and across and soaked in iced water to open into chrysanthemums. It was strange to find many of these onions had been eaten along with the vol-au-vents: 'Quite robust fare for such a group!' There were January king cabbages, formed to contain small white turnips, celery tassels, radish roses, carrot flowers and tomato flowers.

So the royal engagement was announced and the staff at Broadlands were sworn to secrecy after we were told that the first three days of the honeymoon would be spent at Broadlands. We had been summoned to the drawing room, where it was always difficult not to let one's attention wander to the view of the River Test, flowing through the grounds at the foot of the sweep of lawn from the terrace. But this time matters were serious and demanded full attention. Lord and Lady Romsey would leave the house to the honeymoon couple. I would cook for them; Vic, the butler, Rose, the housekeeper, and Bryan, the footman, would look after them. We would all be surrounded by the tightest possible security, which had to be as unobtrusive as possible. Their Royal Highnesses would bring a valet, dresser and detective. The secrecy was so impressed upon us that we had to promise not to tell our families and this became more difficult as the weeks passed and the press claimed to have full details of the honeymoon plans. Just as we were told we could perhaps tell our families, there was a scare when the Queen was frightened by blank shots at the Trooping of the Colour and secrecy was enforced once again. As I shopped in Romsey, the shopkeepers, anxious to know if their commodities might be used, began a barrage of questioning. 'You must know if the honeymoon is to start at Broadlands! Surely you know if the papers say it is to be so.' It was hard to keep a blank expression.

During this time there was to be the first public appearance of Diana, as, with Prince Charles, she was to open the new exhibition of Lord Mountbatten's wartime memorabilia and uniforms. A new museum had been created in the William Mary stable block. There was a buffet and reception held in a large marquee on the lawn and we had been invited to this event. As we moved slowly along to shake hands with everyone, Prince Charles caught sight of me and called out, 'I see they've let Betty out of the kitchen to join us.'

Before the crowds had gathered, a nervous Diana had appeared in the kitchen, looking very striking in a vivid green two piece with striped ribbon trimmings, the white frilled stand-up collar and a request: 'Should I wear a hat?' Everyone was charmed by her appearance and later in the morning the butler's youngest daughter, Samantha, bobbed a courtesy and gave Diana a small bunch of lily of the valley hastily made into a posy. A very simple and spontaneous gesture, the first of the many that were to follow.

Broadlands – May 1981, Princess Diana's first public appearance

All of this put us into a relaxed state for the honeymoon days. There were requests from Charles and Diana on visits to the kitchen, such as could the meals be informal or could they decide almost at the last minute whether they wanted to eat indoors or outdoors. So, despite the many menus with alternatives that I was making out for Lady Romsey's approval, I decided to be as easy-going as possible. My one helper, Doris Phelps, was needed to make substantial food for the security staff and, as the time drew near, I prepared to shut myself away for three days, as visits to Romsey, now full of the world press, were beginning to be rather fraught. There was an offer of £10,000 for any photograph I could take of the couple. The highlight of all the stories circulating in Romsey was that the French team were to put on frogmen outfits, jump from the bridge nearby and swim upstream and surface where the bank faced the bedroom windows.

It was a relief when we were given permission to say that the first part of the honeymoon was to be held at Broadlands. This of course came as something of an anticlimax because the press had known it for many weeks.

The weekends of June and July saw Charles and Diana staying at Broadlands. One Saturday I came into the kitchen to prepare tea and found Diana sitting on the kitchen stool at the table, looking very upset and wishing to talk about the afternoon's polo match. The press had broken through the barriers and surrounded her; it had all got out of control. She fled and came back to Broadlands and the kitchen.

It drew nearer to the day of the wedding and somehow there seemed little worry about the cooking itself. It was dealing with the tensions building up around that seemed more of a problem – security staff moving in and so many people from outside trying to be involved. There were even unsolicited gifts of food arriving: cheeses in decorative baskets, lobsters from a fishmonger in Southampton and a letter from the Norwegian embassy asking if I would give them the recipe for kedgeree, which they understood was to be served at the first breakfast. They asked, 'Is it similar to Norwegian pluk fish?' This was because the *Evening Standard* had announced Mrs Elizabeth Thornton, the cook, would be rising early to prepare a breakfast of kedgeree, bacon, sausages, mushrooms, scrambled eggs, etc.! In fact, what amounted to a country-house shoot breakfast and was rather far from reality. The press had tried very hard to discover my name. They rang all the telephone numbers on the estate and somehow I had emerged as Elizabeth instead of Betty.

The Romseys left the night before the wedding, still rearranging the menu; they were torn between attending the actual ceremony and missing all the excitement in their own home. With relief, we turned to last-minute preparations. Vic checked the TV and video recorder umpteen times, having been asked to record the ceremony. Rose prepared the bedroom and I organised the large meals for the security, now hidden away in the offices across the corridor in the basement. There were going to be lights to illuminate the grounds, security, cameras and there would be guard dogs roaming the grounds, but all was to appear as normal as possible.

We were all up and about very early on the day and hurried to complete household preparations in order to go to the top floor to watch the build-up to the ceremony on the TV in the nursery. I went across the courtyard to our flat during the afternoon and, as I came back to the North Door, I saw that the royal car had arrived and was parked outside the basement entrance. This was ready to meet the newly-weds at Romsey Station and bring them back through the town and the main gates, which would then close and that would be the last shot of them that the cameras could take. Strangely it was the sight of the glass-roofed limousine that suddenly brought everything into reality and I remember thinking with quite a shock, *Betty, you will be cooking the wedding-night meal of Prince Charles.* My uppermost thought then was that if only my parents had been alive, how thrilled they would have been to know that all the interest I had taken in cooking from my early teens during the war had now brought me to this kitchen and this rather special occasion.

As 6 p.m. approached and we were to expect our guests,

we gathered in the butler's pantry to watch a small portable TV to let us know when the car approached the gates. The estate workers were lining the route and when Vic, Rose, Bryan and I came to the front door, there was a ripple of excitement. Then, as we opened the doors, there were a few waves of recognition. Suddenly the car was there: Vic stepped forward to open the door, Bryan to deal with the luggage and I was left in the doorway to make the first greeting. I curtsied and said how pleased we were to welcome their Royal Highnesses; it was a moment of great emotion (now, sadly clouded by present events). But all was excitement at this part of a long and tiring day. They hurried through the hall to watch the recording of the day's events and we settled in to the evening and the dinner. As we had planned during previous weekends, the arrangements were flexible and as it promised to be a warm moonlit evening, it was decided the meal would be set on a table on the terrace under the Portico facing the river. Vic hurried to find a suitable table and everything was prepared for the first meal of the honeymoon.

And so this busy life with Royal visits continued. Detectives would sit at the wooden, scrubbed table in the kitchen for meals, revolvers in holsters laid on the table. Everything was a rush and a bustle here. The bells were ringing from upstairs and one could sense the Queen's arrival even though we were hidden away in the basement. Menus were chosen with care because nothing could be too heavy or rich – salmon was a favourite. The Queen was adept at making a small portion last the same length of time as other people's larger helpings by toying with the food. The timing of these meals had to be followed strictly. John was called in to help in the dining room, so could give first-hand reports. The shoot lunches were held in the business room and were very generous in quantity and variety, but caused conflict because the 'guns' tended to linger over their lunch. Hurrying out one day, Prince Philip stuffed bread rolls into his pockets, saying, 'I'm not missing these.' Princess Anne's dogs – a lurcher and terrier – tended to sprawl in one's path, but staff were told to kick them out of the way.

Another gap in writing; it is now 4 October 1997 – four weeks since the funeral of Princess Diana. Sitting in the warmth of an Indian summer, looking up at the beech trees, those events are too painful to think about.

The workload increased. I spent five weeks in Majorca cooking at a family bungalow. It was humid weather and the air conditioning broke down. There were mosquitoes outside and the most temperamental gas cooker it has been my misfortune to meet inside. There was lots of entertaining to make use of my services. Juan Carlos, (a sculptor living in the next bungalow), and John became best buddies at a drinks party and took over the conversation. The rain came at last! I could work more freely and the cooker seemed less menacing. What a relief to be on the plane home! But it was upsetting to be met by stony-faced silence from Vic and Rose, who thought I had been on some sort of holiday while they had cleared out my kitchen in order for it to be decorated sunshine yellow. There was the popular herb chart, which held everyone's attention. The posters and our noticeboard were still there with appropriate drawings and verses. 'She was a good cook as cooks go and as cooks go, she went!' by Saki and Hilaire Belloc's 'The Vulture'. Oh, what a lesson to us all to only eat at dinner!

Christmas was such a busy week; all the Brabournes were staying. I had time off for New Year and collapsed into bed. The house was open to the public in summer and as I made my way from the flat to the kitchen the queues would be forming across the yard past the Japanese cannon and the mounting block, where the stable girls would have the horses waiting for the royal riders.

BROADLANDS

FAMILY SYNDICATES - SHOOTING SEASON 1980/81

SAT. NOVEMBER 15TH - RIDGE

FAMILY	(1. HRH THE DUKE OF GLOUCESTER	HRH THE DUCHESS OF GLOUCESTER
&	(2. THE DUKE OF ABERCORN	
GUESTS	(3. MR EVELYN DE ROTHSCHILD	MRS EVELYN DE ROTHSCHILD
	(4. LORD ROMSEY	LADY ROMSEY
LET	(5. SIR DONALD GOSLING	
GUNS	(6. MR CLIVE ASTON	
	(7.	
	(8.	

SAT. DECEMBER 6TH - BUSHEYLEASE

FAMILY	(1. HRH THE DUKE OF EDINBURGH	HM THE QUEEN
&	(2. LORD BRABOURNE	COUNTESS MOUNTBATTEN OF BURMA
GUESTS	(3. MR DAVID HICKS	LADY PAMELA HICKS
	(4. LORD ROMSEY	LADY ROMSEY
LET	(5. SIR DONALD GOSLING	
GUNS	(6. MR CLIVE ASTON	
	(7.	
	(8.	

SAT. DECEMBER 13TH - RIDGE

FAMILY	(1. THE HON ANGUS OGILVY	HRH PRINCESS ALEXANDRA
&	(2. MR NICHOLAS PHILLIPS	MRS NICHOLAS PHILLIPS
GUESTS	(3. DR HERBERT KLOIBER	MRS HERBERT KLOIBER
	(4. LORD ROMSEY	LADY ROMSEY
LET	(5. SIR DONALD GOSLING	
GUNS	(6. MR CLIVE ASTON	
	(7. MR HUGH ROSS	
	(8.	

SAT. JANUARY 10TH - RIDGE

FAMILY	(1. HM THE KING OF GREECE	HM THE QUEEN OF GREECE
&	(2. CDR. ROBERT DE PASS	MRS ROBERT DE PASS
GUESTS	(3.	
	(4. LORD ROMSEY	LADY ROMSEY
LET	(5. SIR DONALD GOSLING	
GUNS	(6. MR CLIVE ASTON	
	(7. MR HUGH ROSS	
	(8.	

SAT. JANUARY 24TH - BUSHEYLEASE

FAMILY	(1. CAPTAIN MARK PHILLIPS	HRH PRINCESS ANNE
&	(2. HRH THE DUKE OF KENT	HRH THE DUCHESS OF KENT
GUESTS	(3. DONALD CAMERON YR OF LOCHIEL	LADY CECIL CAMERON
	(4. LORD ROMSEY	LADY ROMSEY
LET	(5. SIR DONALD GOSLING	
GUNS	(6. MR CLIVE ASTON	

The guest list for the shooting season 1980/81

I managed to fit in driving lessons at this time, aged fifty-seven! I would see the driving instructor's car, bright pea green, making its way up the park and would try to reach him before he came into the stable yard. Otherwise it gave much amusement to passing gardeners, builders and general public queuing for the exhibition, to watch my departure – they were just waiting for me to stall or miss a gear. We headed for the Shirley district of Southampton, many times in fact. It all became slightly surreal for the instructor when I had to cancel one test because HM the Queen was coming for tea that day!

On test days – three in all – I would walk halfway down the park and step out from behind a tree to halt the car. Perhaps this was my version of the emergency stop! Secrecy meant I didn't have to answer to 'Did you pass then?' on the occasions when I hadn't!

Seven

In September 1982, I decided to look for another job – and so another kitchen. We came to Bighton House, Cadbury territory. Our new home was a thatched cottage at the entrance to the drive, with woods all round and deer in the garden; it all seemed idyllic. But this was to prove a very difficult seven months.

The cottage kitchen was a wooden hut-like extension and had a smoky Rayburn stove, which was difficult to cook on. The kitchen of Bighton House had been designed by the lady of the house, Mrs Wigan – a strong personality and an organiser. A large ledger lay open on one table; we had to record all happenings of the day and the menus. The nursery was across the corridor and everyday meals were taken in an annexe to the kitchen. An open area above a cupboard enabled me to pass the food through and clear away. Three small boys and their nanny would sit along a high-backed settle facing the table. There was always much fighting and kicking. Outside the French window there was a play area with wire fencing, known to us all as 'Colditz'. The children spent much time playing out here and I was asked to keep an eye on them.

I shared the kitchen with a parrot in a large brass cage, two budgies in a cage alongside his and three dogs. One of these dogs was a Great Dane. The parrot had appeared on television in commercials, but had, at one stage, got overheated by the lights and had given someone a nasty peck so that was the end of that. One Labrador was Mrs Wigan's and had appeared in the wedding photographs. The other old Labrador was Mr Wigan's and was called

Moss. He was meant to travel each day to the office of the hop business owned by the Wigan family, near Tower Bridge. Poor Moss had been disciplined in his early days by a gamekeeper and never barked because the punishment was to be bitten on his ears. He begged for titbits with his eyes, but was forbidden to eat any. To my embarrassment, a half sausage I once made him accept was carried in his mouth all day and dropped at Mr Wigan's feet on his return.

There was entertaining every weekend. Mr Wigan took Friday off and spent the day at the cash and carry. I pushed the trolley alongside him, for food, while he bought the drink. Home-made potato crisps were the order of the day. We seemed to have artichokes on the menu many times and always spinach as these came from the garden and we were a very economical household.

The washers and washing machine only ran at night on economy and the ice-making machine was switched off as soon as the need for ice ceased in the evening. We switched lights on and off, probably using more power than leaving them on would have done.

There were guests every weekend as it was unthinkable that there should be a Saturday evening or Sunday lunch-time without people. Often there were last-minute phone calls to obtain guests.

As staff we were a mixed crew. My helper in the evening, Sue, came from a local gypsy family, but was eager to learn and conquered the difficulty of not knowing right from left by saying, 'Wristwatch on the left and forks on the left.' A family, who were soon to leave under mysterious circum-stances, lived in an upstairs flat. The mother talked of being the Wigans' old nanny, despite only having been there a couple of years! Two sons gardened and looked after two horses. A butler came in only when required and was, in fact, a local council worker and occasional ambulance man. He also drove the gritting machine, so during the winter months was often called out if frost was forecast and sent a friend instead. This didn't help for smooth running in the kitchen.

Christmas had to be arranged around family feuds. Sir Peter Cadbury would not be in the house at the same time as his ex-wife; the older Wigans (a delightful couple – Derek Wigan entertaining the boys with conjuring and magic) did not care to dine with the Cadburys. A very uneasy atmosphere pervaded this household. Soon after Christmas my troubles began: the Great Dane died, unfortunately when Mrs Wigan was away. The nanny and I found him in his giant bed-like basket, lined with a sable wrap, quite dead, at the foot of the stairs. Breaking the news was difficult and the tears and reproaches went on for days. His burial place was altered twice and gloom hung over the house. Then Sir P Cadbury decreed that there must be a new puppy to heal the situation and this gangly youngster entered the kitchen, quite like a young calf. He was to have his basket by the Aga, adding to my difficulties as regarding animal and bird life in the kitchen. Many times when stirring sauces I would pick out soft budgie down, tiny feathers or the occasional sunflower seed flicked from the parrot's cage. The newcomer was christened Chutney after a butler in an America cartoon and I became adept at stepping over him. Then he had hard-paid injections and nearly died. Not house-trained at this point, the resultant mess in the kitchen was disastrous. But when I was told I must clear it up before starting to cook breakfast, I rebelled and said the situation was totally unhygienic and I couldn't do it. My punishment started. I was told I must let the dogs out and walk them round the garden, and if I wouldn't clear the mess, the children couldn't be expected to eat in the kitchen. So I had to undo the shutters in the dining room, set the table there and carry the breakfast through. The smell from the kitchen was already turning my stomach as I opened up the back door in the mornings. Life became difficult. My helper Sue walked out in the middle of a dinner party, telling me, 'It will be your turn next. You'll be gone in a week!'

Sure enough it was a case of 'as cooks go, she went'. It was a Saturday lunchtime and the atmosphere was impossible so, with great satisfaction, I walked down the corridor to the back door, wheeled my moped out of the barn, put on my helmet and set off down the drive. I left John to return and add a few pithy remarks to mine.

Trudi Hurst at Mrs Lines' Agency came to the rescue and sent details of jobs she thought would be useful.

Sadly we had to sell the large wooden shed, bought from a building site, which we had put up in the garden as a studio. Painted dark green and lined with stage felt, it was our proud possession. An advert brought many phone calls and it was something we made an excellent profit on.

There was the usual feeling of being disorientated when considering jobs. Should it be Campden House, Chipping Campden or Burghclere, near Newbury? There was a house near World's End, Dorset, Henrietta Tiarks at Woburn or the Duchess of Kent – where would the next kitchen be?

Then Trudi was saying over the phone, 'Stoke-on-Trent? Well, it's more Ashbourne, Derbyshire actually. In fact, JCB excavators in Rocester.' I had long conversations with Carole Bamford and I seemed to be giving so many reasons why I didn't want to live in the Midlands, but was drawn all the time to the voice.

An interview was arranged. We had an 8 a.m. departure only to find the car had been broken into and the spare wheel stolen. Sue's family were well known for this activity, but I did think they could have spared us this, we were waiting outside a local car-breaker's yard at 8.15 a.m. When it opened we were able to buy a spare tyre and start the journey. So onwards to Brownhills, Lichfield, then Uttoxeter. We went off course here and through Cheadle;

we were hungry as we came down a steep hill into Oakamoor, but there was a sign, 'The Admiral Jervis'. This was soon to become so familiar to us as our local eating place. We were rather late for lunch but everyone was kind; Nora behind the bar was anxious to give directions, being mother-in-law to the gardener at Farley Hall, the very place we needed to be. I was so conscious of this very different landscape – not the softness of Hampshire but almost as familiar as Yorkshire. Again up a steep hill, a sharp turn, stables to one side of the road and a black and white hall with a solarium to the left. We had problems with the electric gate, but I couldn't think why afterwards.

So finally we came along the front of the house, rang a bell and a slim, blonde, tanned figure wearing navy and white let us in and so we came to safe waters after stormy passages. Words came easily. Photographs of the children interrupted the serious business of interviewing. Anthony Bamford came into the room smiling. We spoke of Robin Compton, known to them both, and of Bill Hughes. When I spoke of £60 as my wage at that time, they said, 'Well, let's say £70,' which seemed a generous start.

The journey back to Bighton seemed much shorter than the morning's drive, for there was much to discuss as we had looked round Farley Lodge, which would be where we would live if we came to Farley. Sensibly, it had been agreed that we should return for a second interview; our heads were spinning with all the new impressions and details.

How strange, in these first moments of an interview and after the introduction, 'Yes, I'm Betty Thornton, sent by the Lines' Agency and this is my husband, John.' There is so much about to unfold. But you are unaware of it at the time and do not see ahead to the new routine, the shared experiences – this will be your new place of work, but so much more. Your own family will visit and gradually become known to everyone in the household.

To pick up the thread again, there was a second interview, part of which took place in the factory. We had a meal in the canteen, overlooked by a stuffed giraffe, and then an interlude in the theatre to see an audio-visual show of the famous machinery. Surely not many cooks have had such an unusual interview! We had a tour of the estate and then went to see the Lodge close to the black and white house on the hill. Within a month, the removal men were bringing the goods and chattels from Hampshire to Staffordshire.

The new routine could now begin, hampered a little by the fact that removals always rob this cook of her voice – it must be the dust.

Planning for dinner parties settled into a familiar pattern, all leading to that exciting moment when guests would arrive. But before that happened there would have been breakfast at 7.45 a.m. for the three children and their nanny, followed by Anthony Bamford's breakfast and his departure for the JCB factory. His office was in touch with the world – a helicopter on the pad, a jet at the nearby airport and a fleet of cars standing by.

At the black and white house on the hill, Carole Bamford and the household were kept busy. Flowers were brought in from the garden and the house slowly filled with arrangements. The sculptor-cum-butler cleaned silver and his white gloved hands carefully arranged candelabra and centrepieces on the table. The cook tried to achieve as much preparation as possible during the morning – fresh fish was delivered from Mr Room's in Derby, other specials from London – Justin de Blanks, Fortnums and Harrods. It was all brought in a chauffeur-driven car and all taken care of by the most efficient chauffeur-shopper one could wish for – Kenneth Bradley, known as Brad, who could anticipate, substitute, read the cook's mind and never failed.

The phone would ring: 'I am in Sainsbury's and they haven't got the brand you wanted, shall I get such and such? By the way, I think you needed a new packet of Cheerios this week!'

Carole Bamford and I would work together on vegetable preparation, chatting happily. The groom from the stables, who was to become the footman in the evening, called in to be briefed. Time for a light lunch – I would then hurry home along the front terrace for a short break. At 4 p.m. the children would arrive home for tea. The TV would be on in the breakfast annexe and homework was done at the Mouse Thompson table, often well into the evening.

For a memorable period, and for the second time in my cooking days, a parrot shared the kitchen with us. His name was Puffy and his cage hung from an ornate bracket made by the factory carpenter. Sadly he was a bad-tempered parrot and spent a lot of time in the evenings covered by a cloth because the more chattering and bustle in the kitchen, the more squawking came from Puffy. He was sent to Alton Towers, just down the road, for training in good behaviour by the parrot man whose own parrots, appearing before the public, were quiet and well behaved. They performed on the high wire and roller-skated without complaint. Sadly Puffy came back unrepentant and noisier than ever. Our groom-cum-footman was reluctant to admit fear of anything, but avoided feeding and cleaning duties whenever possible.

Like the stage lights going up before a performance, the theatre humming with activity and the audience filing in, so the house took on a very special atmosphere on a party night. The three children delayed bedtime for as long as possible, looking so clean and angelic in dressing gowns and slippers. The lamps were switched on, their scented rings adding to the perfume of the flowers, heavy curtains were drawn across the windows and the log fires were lit. If drinks were to be served in the library, Anthony Bamford, Carole Bamford and the sculptor-cum-butler adjourned there, having called in at the kitchen first. Then everything was ready for the first guests to arrive. Sometimes they would say, 'Just time to open some champagne; light a cigarette.' All three would settle on the fender for a few moments, then the bell would ring at the hall door and everything was greeting, conversation and the warmest hospitality.

I was in the kitchen poised and waiting for those words, 'Everyone in the dining room ready to go!' The trolley was by the Aga waiting to be loaded with the first plates to be taken along the corridor. The butler had taken on his role of quiet efficiency, while I was still slightly temperamental until the main course was safely in. The pudding plates, usually sixteen, were assembled on the long wooden table for final decoration. Then: bliss, a feeling of relaxation and euphoria, especially if the messages from the dining room were favourable. Also it was possible to pick up on the laughter and buzz of conversation to determine the success of a meal. Then we had drinks for everyone in the kitchen and our staff supper.

Onwards then to the washing-up and careful handling of the wine glasses. When the floor was finally swept and mopped and the black plastic bags carried outside, it would be nearly midnight. Cars would be waiting on the terrace and sometimes we would all gather together in the kitchen again to discuss the success of the evening. Then it was home again along the terrace, passing the Cedar of Lebanon tree. Owls hooting, I would open the small gate leading to the drive of the Lodge and finally sink into bed feeling it was a well-earned rest.

At 7.30 a.m., I had a brisk walk back along the terrace, it seeming only a short time since the previous evening. I took a short cut through the boiler house and into the kitchen. I quickly got back into routine – Aga lids lifted, kettle on, Aga tennis-bat toaster charged with bread, oranges taken from the large wooden bowl on the dresser. These were two per person and they were squeezed on the Braun juice extractor. Once a mechanically minded two-year-old deftly dismantled this while my back was turned and handed the spindle to me with a disarming smile. Sausages were placed in the oven, the bacon snipped, a pan for poached eggs and a pan for boiled eggs got out, Sister Bridget's butter – a present from Skibareen – ready to spread. There was porridge if required and a battalion of cornflake packets on the table. A cafetière was warming at the back of the Aga and everything was ready. Breakfast over, there was a last-minute dash for the car across the cobbled yard. Then Anthony Bamford's breakfast – newspapers folded, post on the table and sometimes the magic words, 'Your day off tomorrow, passports in order?' What bliss – an outing to Paris!

There was one day off per week and it was put to good use with outings to Ashbourne, Derby and Matlock. Here we visited Gulliver's Kingdom with my grandchildren. In Romford we saw the Mill, Arkwright's Spinning Jenny and a Factory Shop. We went to Uttoxeter for the Dr Johnson Memorial and also its fine cinema. We saw Haddon, Chatsworth, Wirkworth, Gawsthorpe, Capesthorne, Mowcop, Congleton, Leek and Rudyard Lake. We also went further afield to Shrewsbury, Hardwick, Southwell and into neat-and-tidy Cheshire for visits to Styal Mill, but also Chester itself. Sometimes Tuesday evening would be free, giving extra time, and we would leave late afternoon and stay overnight in a B&B. There was time spent in a farm-house at Clun, a pub at Church Enstone and a bungalow in Chipping Norton, never guessing that in 1988, instead of visiting it as an old wool town, it would become our local shopping town. It still had an air of hippy or traveller about it, perhaps because of the influence of the ancient Rollright Stones nearby. These formed a circle and it was said to be impossible to count the same number of stones each time. Recently sold, at the time the circle was owned by Pauline Flick, who also ran a cat sanctuary. The chief cat, to be seen peeping round the stones, was Stray Boy, rescued from London.

The kitchen saw many different activities and eventing became important in the children's lives. The night before an event, three baskets were placed in the hallway containing their velvet-covered riding hats (gradually changing in size as the years went by), gloves, ribbons, crops and handkerchiefs. There was an early call if there was a long drive, perhaps to Malvern or Builth Wells, which we had all mispronounced as Bulth Wells in early days and never could get it right. I would be in early to prepare a picnic – mostly hearty food, with one or two different items as a surprise – always a good idea when preparing a picnic. There were sausages, soup in the wide-mouthed thermos, flapjack, fruit cake, crisps, biscuits, fruit for the adults, wine in the cooler box, individual quiches, slices of savoury meat roll, smoked salmon and cheeses. The list then had to be checked and the bottle opener, wine glasses, fruit knife, kitchen roll and newspapers all had to be carried out to the camper. Then it was 'Wagons roll' and a sigh of relief in the kitchen.

Summer saw picnics on the estate near the Temple or a Sunday barbecue on the front lawn. The most memorable was the one transferred into the hall porch because of heavy rain, while Anthony Bamford and the butler concentrated on turning over sausages and chicken pieces, oblivious to the smoke that was filling the house. Easter was the time for the egg hunt in the garden, followed by games of French cricket with a grandfather who never seemed to tire. Those on the top deck of coaches passing the house on their way to

Alton Towers enjoyed a glimpse of all these activities. They were surprised to see evening drinks being set out in the solarium by a butler carrying his silver tray and more surprised if the helicopter was coming in to land on the terrace.

The kitchen was to be redesigned and so for some time the cooking was done in the back kitchen, near the laundry and larder. It was a very small area, which called for ingenuity and something of the wartime spirit of 'make do and mend'. The trolley containing the food was wheeled down two corridors and often wheeled back by Anthony Bamford to the words and music of Casey Jones's 'Coming Down the Track'.

Birthdays were a challenge to produce a cake appropriate to the interests of the child in question. A favourite was Snoopy, lying on his back with a glass of lemonade at his side and a sandwich in his paw, saying, 'Have a bite with me!' There was a speedway track with cars crossing over bridges and under viaducts; it was rather difficult to stop the almond-paste roads from sagging after an hour or two.

This was happy cooking, blending family needs and formal food. I made lemon refresher, lots of jam, the Robert Carrier rich chocolate cake, the favourite orange cake, liver Dubonnet and, always on return from holiday, cheese pie.

Sunday lunch was served in the dining room for the children and family to welcome visiting grandparents and for the butler to carve the joint and serve the meal with due formality. As the meal progressed and he made his way round the table, there would be the opportunity for him to introduce a short talk on Roman civilisation – a little unusual for a family enjoying their roast pork or chicken. After the meal the children would recite poems and the trolley would not be returned to the kitchen in time for the coffee because the butler would be delivering, 'Once more into the breach, dear friends, once more!'

John and I would leave the tea trolley set with sandwiches and cake and wend our way home to rest, having had our Sunday lunch at the kitchen table looking out on to the Churnet Valley. This kitchen saw the comings and goings of many different people as the courtyard which it overlooked was the entry to the house and messages were often passed through the kitchen window, as were the milk and cream churns each morning. The ponies were often ridden into the yard to be admired and racing cars and vintage cars were brought out of the garages to be tuned up and tested. There were also interesting deliveries from London of flowers, food, antiques and designer clothes.

Now it was 1988 and there were thoughts of retirement for the cook but there was to be one more working kitchen, this time in Gloucestershire. The family from the black and white house on the hill were going to move to a house built in the eighteenth century for Warren Hastings, first governor of Bengal, and I was to still cook for them. Warren Hastings had endured a seven-year trial of impeachment, but was to spend the last years of his life on this peaceful estate, bringing to it a touch of India in ivory furniture, silk drapes and tropical plants for the kitchen garden. Sadly the yak he brought didn't survive.

The kitchen was in need of alteration, but would remain as it was for some time until the rest of the work on the house was well under way. So it would see some busy times with preparation of food for all the designers, technical teams, consultants and most of all for the family, on their many visits getting to know their new surroundings. Gradually, as the house was altered, new floors laid, rewiring done and the plumbing brought up to date, the kitchen became inaccessible and the working lunches were prepared and served in many different places – in grand rooms, in basements, in small rooms tucked away, in the staff area and outside on warm days. Trays were carried across planking with gaps to the floors below and a birthday lunch was held in an all-but-empty room with footsteps resounding on bare floorboards, but it was just as jolly as always.

The house had been occupied by American troops shortly before D-Day and so a visit by an ex-US Army war veteran gave us a vivid picture of how it looked at that time. The sergeants' bunks had been in the garden room, where post-war Lord Rothermere enjoyed reading his newspapers. The officers had slept in the gallery and morning parade had been held before the open front door (where initials can still be seen scratched into the pillars).

He told us it was a bitterly cold Christmas morning and the men stood in line outside the mess huts at the back of the house; the sergeants were allowed to carry their meal back into the house.

I wonder what Warren Hastings would have thought of all this if he could have been brought to the twentieth century. Forty-five years after the troops, there would be another large mess hut and Portaloos for the builders working on the house.

There would be decorative reminders of this man added to the house that I am sure he would have approved of. There were elephants on the foot scrapers, the work of John, and on the lead tanks. His beautiful orangery was looked after and so many of his personal belongings brought back to the house.

Conclusion

During all this time, the preparation and serving of food has been my whole life. From first making bread in a Leeds kitchen in the '30s, learning how to make lentil soup and apple dumplings in Domestic Science lessons at school, through wartime shortages, to the final return of good food after the war and the mounting interest in cookery in all its aspects shown by everyone.

I marvel that repetition, flag as it will at times, can always challenge the person in the kitchen and can call forth surprise after surprise. This creativity and skill, sometimes only hurriedly acquired upon the setting-up of a household, blossoms and improves with that very repetition. It is hard to believe that such responsibility to nurture and sustain, such time-consuming work should call out the willingness to return, at least three times a day, to the kitchen. When true poverty was prevalent among large families there were mothers, surely gifted, who could make satisfying meals from the most basic foodstuff. They could make a suet pudding, boiled in a cloth in a pan over the fire, with small pieces of meat added or turnip or peas that would fill the stomach and satisfy the taste of a brood of children. The cook is always the mother figure and her greatest satisfaction and pleasure is to serve food at that very moment when the recipient is at their hungriest, eager for food. At the other end of the scale is the frustration of serving food to anyone bored, well sated and ready to criticise food which is deserving of praise and appreciation. It is our very lifeline, our existence and is perhaps summed up in the lines:

We may live without poetry, music and art,
We may live without conscience and live without
 heart;
We may live without friends, we may live
 without books,
But civilised man cannot live without cooks!

Edward Bulmer, Earl of Lytton (1831–1891)

And now, what of the cook and the sculptor-butler? They have reached their seventies, celebrated their golden wedding anniversary and live in a garden cottage. Meals, just for two, are prepared here, in a kitchen overlooking a greenhouse and an orchid house, with a glimpse of the mellow bricks of the eighteenth-century kitchen garden wall.

They sit at their table and sometimes talk of the war years, of post-war London and sometimes of the farm men that they knew – Will Cranstoun, Tom Thackeray, the gypsy, Charlie Brown from Wath-on-Dearne, 'Dinks' Needham, 'Ben-Hur' Smith and Wally Hammond. They talk of the stately home open days, when the day's schedule was read eagerly by the guides to discover unusual names or titles of groups – such as the afternoon of the Reverend Stalker and Mrs Corker and 'The Autumn Leaves'. They recall dinner parties and shooting parties, power failures at the crucial moments of preparing and serving a meal. They think of two children waiting at the top of the stairs leading to the flat in the Robert Adam wing, waiting for the magic word – 'leftovers'. The days of Jenkins and Auntie Amy bring a smile and they still shiver at the memory of that desperately cold winter of '62 in Westmoreland.

They have three grandchildren – Lucy, Amy and Louis, who share life at the cottage on weekend visits.

When they think of their days as art students and first

meeting aged sixteen and seventeen, they like to imagine with what utter disbelief they would have greeted this story of cooking, waiting on table and farm work. But they know that sculpture, history and their own love would provide a thread that bound and held it all together. Such a melange, but an excellent recipe and a meal to be savoured. Perhaps humour was one of the most important ingredients.

★

John died in August 2003 and Betty returned to Yorkshire to live in a flat whose windows look across to Baildon Moor, where they walked together.

2004: Betty, sixty years on
Taken by Stanley Searle APAGB, Bedford Photography Club

Lightning Source UK Ltd.
Milton Keynes UK
08 February 2010
149758UK00001B/2/P

9 781847 486172